Praise for Paul Ferrini's Books

"The most important book I have read. I study it like a bible!" Elisabeth Kubler-Ross, M.D.

"These words embody tolerance, universality, love and compassion—hallmarks of all Great Teachings. They turn our attention inward to our own divine nature, instead of diverting it outward. Paul Ferrini is a modern-day Kahlil Gibran—poet, mystic, visionary, teller of truth." Larry Dossey, M.D.

"Paul Ferrini leads us skillfully and courageously beyond shame, blame and attachment to our wounds into the depths of self-forgiveness. His work is a must-read for all people who are ready to take responsibility for their own healing." John Bradshaw

"A breath of fresh air in an often musty and cluttered domain. With sweetness, clarity, and simplicity we are directed to the truth within. I read this book whenever my heart directs, which is often." Pat Rodegast

"Paul Ferrini's writing is authentic, delightful and wise. It reconnects the reader to the Spirit Within, to that place where even our deepest wounds can be healed." Joan Borysenko, Ph.D.

"I feel that this work comes from a continuous friendship with the deepest part of the Self. I trust its wisdom." Coleman Barks, poet and translator.

"Paul Ferrini's wonderful books show a way to walk lightly with joy on planet earth." Gerald Jampolsky, M.D.

"Paul Ferrini leads us on a gentle journey to our true source of joy and happiness—inside ourselves." Ken Keyes, Jr.

Cover Design by Aryeh Swisa
Book Design by Elizabeth Lewis
Typesetting by Michael Gray
Wounded Child painting and line drawings based on crest design
motifs by Rosemary Ladd-Griffin

ISBN 1-879159-06-6

Second Edition: June, 1997

The Wounded Child's
Journey
into Love's Embrace

Paul Ferrini

PREFACE TO THE SECOND EDITION

Readers will note that I have decided to use my previous subtitle *The Wounded Child's Journey into Love's Embrace* as the primary title for this second edition. The previous title *The Circle of Atonement* refers to a specific concept from *A Course in Miracles* which may not be familiar to many readers. While the *Course* remains an important part of my background, knowledge of it is not a prerequisite for understanding this or any of my books.

This book looks at the practical day to day applications of the universal teachings of love and forgiveness, as presented by Jesus and other masters. It contains many examples from my own life experience and encourages you to look at your own life as the primary subject matter for your spiritual growth.

Each one of us has within our consciousness a wounded little child who does not feel that s/he is lovable. That child is fearful, hurt, suspicious, angry, withdrawn, resentful, judgmental, fault-finding, you name it. S/he was not offered unconditional love and s/he therefore does not know how to offer it to self or others. The whole ego structure with its elaborate defense mechanisms has been built to protect that child from perceived/anticipated trespass or violation.

It is impossible to experience wholeness in the psyche — which is what spirituality means — without learning to love and accept this wounded being within our own consciousness. The spiritual adult and the wounded child must establish an ongoing dialogue if our thoughts, feelings and actions are going to be congruent with our spiritual beliefs.

Our connection to Love within our hearts enables us to accept ourselves even when we make mistakes. It helps us take responsibility for our thoughts and actions when we feel hurt, wounded, or victimized by another person. And it enables us to abandon our judgments and make amends when we have attacked another person. These are all essential steps in the healing process.

We have all searched for love outside of ourselves. But we did not find it there. The truth is, Love must be discovered within our own hearts, in the midst of our pain. We are the bringers of light. But before we can bring light to any one else, we must first find it within the shadowy, secret places of our own psyche.

This book was written to help you learn to listen to the fearful, fault-finding, tantrumming child within who withdraws or attacks when s/he doesn't get what s/he wants. By befriending that child, and learning to hold him or her in a compassionate way, you bridge the gap between dark and light, ego and spirit.

This is a work of great courage. If you stay with it, you cannot fail to find the place within where you are connected to love and guided by your own light.

Namaste

Paul Ferrini
June, 1997

To The Reader

This book is a sequel to my previous book *The Bridge To Reality*. While that earlier work focused on self-forgiveness as the key to inner peace, this book focuses on the extension of our peace in creative work and relationship with others. Both books discuss a healing process in which we overcome shame, learn from our mistakes, and take responsibility for creating a life of joy and integrity.

Through this process, we begin to discover the divine Spirit that lives in all of us. We accept ourselves and others more deeply and begin to find new opportunities to work creatively and in harmony with others. By deepening our self-acceptance, we intensfiy our joy so that it naturally extends to others. We offer our abundance to all who would share it, inviting everyone into the circle of grace. This is the ongoing process of the At-one-ment.

Although this book draws upon my experience as a teacher and student of *A Course in Miracles* it is accessible to you regardless of your background. Emphasizing the universal teachings common to many spiritual traditions, *The Circle of Atonement* offers you a spiritual practice that you can integrate into your daily life. It will inspire you as you open your heart to others and to God.

PREFACE

We do not find our way into the circle of healing by denying our pain or running away from it. We must acknowledge our pain and move through it. Our pain is there for a reason. It has come to tell us that we feel separate and we don't want to feel separate any more. It has come to tell us that love is what we want.

The circle of healing begins in our own hearts. It extends from the depths of hell to the heights of heaven. There is no place where it does not reach. There is no sadness it does not uplift, no lack that it does not abundantly address. But we must find the circle within before we can extend it to others. We must learn to love and accept ourselves and then share that love with those who are close to us. The more we love, the more the circle opens. In the end, there is no one who stands outside it. That is the Atonement.

The potential for peace is already here. We just need to allow it. We just need to feel its presence in our hearts.

Everyone has a special part to play in the Atonement, but the message given to each one is always the same: God's Son is guiltless. Each one teaches the message differently, and learns it differently. Yet until he teaches it and learns it, he will suffer the pain of dim awareness that his true function remains unfulfilled in him . . . From everyone you accord release from guilt you will inevitably learn your innocence. The circle of Atonement has no end. And you will find ever-increasing confidence in your safe inclusion in the circle with everyone you bring within its safety and its perfect peace.

A COURSE IN MIRACLES; TEXT
pp. 262 and 263.

TABLE OF CONTENTS

Part One

Opening the Way of the Heart

MOVING INTO THE HEART

God wants us to be vulnerable. In our vulnerability, we open like a flower. We channel the divine energy into the shape of our lives.

My friend Carol is especially open. She stays with her feelings. She speaks of her discomfort, her feelings of separation from others in our group. We all feel separate in the same way. But it is harder for us to own our feelings of separateness.

By owning her feelings, she helps us all own ours. Now there is a different energy in the group. Now, somehow, we have become more real. We have sunk down into the heart. We are with our fears. And it feels okay. Yes, it is okay to feel our separateness. It is honest. Feeling our separateness is more real than pretending it isn't there.

When I hear that my sister is afraid, I feel compassion, for I too am afraid. I know what she feels in my own heart. The walls of separation come down. She is vulnerable and so am I. We are both children, sharing our fears. But now there is no parent to fix things for us, or to demand that we come up out of our feelings. Now there is only our witness to each other, as brother and sister.

There was a time when being together in this way was not possible for our group. When someone spoke about their pain, everyone jumped in and tried to fix it. And the "fixing" was like an attack against the one sharing. Now, it is different. Now, we are learning how to use each other's witness to go within.

As I take what you say through my own heart, I emerge feeling closer to you. Your honesty and vulnerability invite me "in," but not into you. They invite me into myself, where I join with you. I allow myself to find the level of inner truth in what you say. I understand that what you say is not about you only, but also about me.

The state of love communion is simply this state of joining within with another, heart to heart. It is not an experience of the other as "other" or as object. It is an experience of the other as myself.

It does not require a movement toward that person for satisfaction, for there is already joining present. Nothing needs to be added to it.

When I meet you in my own heart, there is nowhere else I have to go. As long as we both remain in our hearts, our joining continues. When we move out of our hearts, we simply move away. And coming together does not mean reaching out after you, but reaching within myself to find the place where we are connected.

HEGEMONY OF THE HEAD

Feeling separate from you is just a symptom of feeling separate from myself. I am in my head, in my intellect, in my ego. And so I see you as an object that moves away from me, or toward me. And I want you to move a certain way, so the whole direction of my being, my whole attention is externalized.

When I am in my head, I expect certain results. My happiness depends on securing certain behaviors from you. I am like a general on the battlefield, marshaling the troops, conducting endless strategy meetings. "If this happens, I'll do that. If that happens, I'll do this."

I become thought bound. When I am thought bound, I forget my body. I become ungrounded. Thus, my strategies, though a marvel to behold, are totally ineffective in accomplishing my objectives. For my objectives are primarily objectives for the body, and it is the body from which I have become dis-engaged.

When I stay in the heart, something else happens. I reach to you through myself. This is extension. If you move away, I do not feel abandoned. I simply sense your fear and honor your need for boundaries with me. My love for you emanates from my love for myself. It is full already. It does not need you to fill it up.

The kind of love that needs to be filled up is the general's love. His need for external results comes from a consciousness of lack. It says "I will not be happy unless this happens or that happens." It says "my happiness is conditional on the way that you respond to me." It is an emptiness that reaches out to be filled.

It is not that the general does not feel. He does. But since he disconnected himself from his feelings, he does not know "what" or "how" he feels. The only way he can experience his feelings is through others.

Feeling, for the general, is unconscious. It is his id, his instinct, his sexuality. It is impersonal for him, so he takes no responsibility for it. To him "feelings happen" in relationship to someone else. The woman (or man if the general is a woman) draws him out, and turns him inside out. Feelings erupt, but he feels that she is responsible for them.

By projecting his feelings, the general lives a "charmed" life. To everyone else he seems to have his life together. Everything in his life is handled. Even what isn't handled is arranged so perfectly it seems to be handled.

Meanwhile inside the general's heart is PAIN, and SELF-LOATHING. By externalizing his feelings, he is not in charge of meeting his needs. Sure, he is in charge of meeting everyone else's needs. But here he is, this strong man (or woman), and he is totally dependent on others to get his needs met.

Boys are always practicing to be generals, but when they finally become generals they forget how to be boys. They forget to cry, to feel their pain.

Interestingly, when his armor cracks and the tears begin to flow, the general disappoints a lot of people. They see that he will not be able to carry them any more and they move away from him. They find other generals to carry them. Perhaps a few who really love him remain to hold his hand. But, lacking them, the general weeps alone.

❂

CO-DEPENDENCY

Our social institutions and economic order are the creations of generals and general-makers. We must remember that for every general, there is at least one general-maker.

Generals want to control life. They like to make decisions, but they are afraid of their feelings. They trade their feelings for control.

General-makers are beset with contradictory feelings. They are afraid to decide, and prefer to let the general decide for them. They trade their power for security.

Before the women's movement, men staked out the role of general. Now women claim it too. It is not just a male-female issue. It is a power issue.

When the general can't handle his self imposed burden of responsibility, he rebounds into addictive, self-destructive behavior. He goes out of control in some way. He becomes an alcoholic or a drug addict or perhaps he loses all his money. He impulsively sheds the cloak of responsibility. "Now it's time for you to take care of me," he says.

And so perhaps the roles shift. The one who was taken care of becomes the caretaker.

There are many variations on this theme. Often the roles are not so clearly spelled out. But the issues of control and powerlessness are always there. Somewhere, in our relationships, there is an unwritten agreement that starts out as: "You do this and I'll do that" and soon becomes "If you don't do this, I won't do that."

At some point, we take a look at our lives and realize that neither we, nor our partners, are actualizing ourselves. We are stuck in roles that might have made sense once, but don't make sense any more.

The roles we agree to play are developmental. They help us gain confidence and learn our lessons. Once the lessons have been learned, the roles are no longer necessary.

The freedom from roles is one way that we remove unnecessary limits in our lives. Growth means moving beyond what we no longer need.

Generals must learn to follow their hearts. They must learn to let go and let others contribute. General makers must learn to decide and act for themselves. They must learn to take responsibility.

Ultimately we are here to integrate heart and mind, reason and feeling. We are here to learn to give and to receive. There is nothing wrong with taking care of others if we let others take care of us. There is nothing wrong in leading if we can also follow.

Ours is an experiment in equality and mutuality. Anything short of that causes imbalance and pain. Our lessons are all about coming out of that pain and imbalance. They help us see where the inequality is. For wherever there is too much, somewhere else there is a scarcity.

All our spiritual lessons are about balance. That's why Buddha called his teaching "the Middle Way." There will always be extremes, but extremes just teach us pain. Our work is to harmonize those extremes in our own life, in our own consciousness.

That reconciliation brings inner peace. And from that peace, joy spontaneously flows.

✪

THE DESCENT INTO HELL

A large part of our journey is about embracing our own darkness. We don't get to heaven unless we have walked through hell.

Many belief systems promise short cuts. By promising light and denying the darkness, they may postpone the descent, but when it comes, as it inevitably does, it is often more devastating.

Neither heaven nor hell exist outside of consciousness. Hell is the place where we are confronted by all our self-judgments. Heaven is the place where we dissolve those judgments in self-forgiveness.

The law of life is simple. I must confront every belief I have about myself. Some of my beliefs are conscious. Many of them are not. Clearly, the subconscious beliefs are the ones that give me the most trouble. They present a side of myself at which I am not anxious to look.

It is not the "reality" of my dark side that needs to be confronted so much as the reality of my belief in it. My shame must be acknowledged if I am to bring the wounded child within me into the light of conscious acceptance.

Lest I do this inner work, I cannot expect grace to come into my life. God is ever prepared to meet me, but He will not do my growth for me. It must remain my responsibility.

When I take that responsibility, I regain my freedom and my power. When I shirk it, I remain powerless and in chains.

What I hate about myself will either be acknowledged or it will be projected onto my brothers and sisters. Acknowledging it diffuses its apparent power and brings it closer to me. When I own it, I begin to integrate it.

Anything I hate seems to hate me back. The part of myself that I have disowned in turn condemns me. I must win this part back simply because it belongs to me and I gave it away.

If I give away part of myself, I give away part of my power. My power, the power of the authentic Self is in all of me, not in this part or that. My power is not in the conscious self or in the unconscious self. It is in the unified Self.

When God looked on His creation and saw that it was good, He affirmed it all. He did not say, "this part is good, but the other part leaves something to be desired." He said without compromise or conditions "it is all good."

Each of us is faced with the need to make the same affirmation about ourselves. That is what the descent into hell and the ascent to heaven is all about.

I don't find out about my dark side to agree with its condemnation of me, but to welcome it back, to retrieve its power. As long as it stands apart from me, it appears ominous, negative, incapable of redemption. But when I bring it closer, when I embrace it, I begin to see its positive significance.

I begin to see some positive aspect of my selfhood which I prematurely rejected, because I didn't trust it, or because it wasn't valued by others. I called it evil, but it is not evil. It is simply the part of me that doesn't fit the expectations of others. Now I have internalized those expectations, so it is not others who stand in judgment of that part of me. I stand in judgment of myself.

Being split into consciously acceptable and unacceptable aspects wreaks havoc with my sense of confidence in who I am. Ironically, what is most unique in me, what is most controversial, is exactly what I must embrace if I would find my purpose in life. Finding that means facing my fears. It is hard to do. But once I do it, I realize that they reveal a hidden flower.

I make the monsters of my life, inner and outer. It is my definition of what is acceptable and what is not that divides my life and holds my power hostage. Who I really am is not divided, but indivisible and intact.

If I don't meet the monster within, I shall surely meet him without. And that is dangerous ground, because then I shall have difficulty recognizing that he belongs to me.

I cannot begin the ascent to heaven until I have confronted my deepest shame, my darkest beliefs about myself. That moment of confrontation is the turning point.

At that moment, I look at the monster that stands before me and I see that he is made up of my own beliefs about myself. If I can recognize the falsehood of those beliefs, his form dissolves and in its place comes an image of love and peace. But if I still give credence to those beliefs, his form will remain terrifying to me, and I will back away from the confrontation. Then, my descent is not complete.

I become a light-bearer when I have brought love to the darkest places of my psyche. Now my ascent begins with Spirit as my guide. The period of testing has ended. Now the period of service begins.

❂

RECLAIMING THE SHADOW

When I was in my early twenties I met the shadow head on. All through my youth, this creature had been terrifying to me. It started when I was three or four years old and my grandmother told me that, if I wasn't good, the bogeyman would come and get me. "Who is the bogeyman?" I asked her. "He's a bad man," she said. "He comes at night and captures the children who haven't been good and takes them home and eats them."

I remember many restless nights when I hadn't been good, lying on my grandmother's couch in the hall, waiting for the bogeyman to make his appearance. He always did.

It was dark in the hall, occasionally lit by the ghastly glow of approaching car lights that would creep along the hallway wall opposite my bed. I would slip in and out of sleep, waking to faces on the wall. Most of the faces that came were just moderately troublesome. But, when the bogeyman came, he would puff himself up, filling up the whole wall, his face swirling around and finally coming into focus as he reached out to grab me. He was kind of half outlaw, half ghost. He wore a huge ten gallon hat, beneath which his face would change from one terrifying visage to another.

I would see him in my dreams, only to wake up, open my eyes, and see him creeping along the wall. There was no safety. He was inside me and outside too. For years, I would see him coming after me in my dreams and try to scream, but I would be frozen in terror. I could not make a sound.

The power this phantom figure had was amazing. Equally amazing was how quickly and easily he went away when I had conquered my fear of him.

In my early twenties, I met this shadow figure in

a dream. He tried to intimidate me, but I stood my ground. We wrestled for some time without finding any weakness in each other. Finally, we stood face to face. "I'm not afraid of you any more," I said. He looked at me and then walked away.

He has not been back since.

Who is this shadow? He is the personification of my guilt about myself. My grandmother told me I was "bad" and had to be punished and I believed her. The bogeyman was the symbol of my guilt and my punishment rolled into one.

Where does this low opinion about myself come from? It is certainly not something I hold alone. Virtually every person I have met and come to know well has admitted to the same deep down feeling of unworthiness, no matter how successful he or she might be on the outside.

Is it a conditioned response to our upbringing, the result of not meeting our parents expectations of us, and consequent feelings of failure or shame? Is it our parents' shame projected onto us? Certainly that has to be part of it. Yet it seems to reach further into our psyches.

Indeed, our guilt has not only a collective, but an ontological significance. It is intricately bound up in our mortality. My deep set belief is that "If I must die, then I must be bad." Death is seen as the punishment for my transgressions. My fear of death and my guilt run hand in hand.

Who is this shadow? He is none other than the grim reaper, the face of death come to meet us. He has the power to take our lives or spare them. He comes to punish us when we haven't been good. He is the dark side of the Godhead — our fear of ourselves projected outward onto some phantom figure who seems to control our fate.

In reality, he has no power at all. We give him all the power he has.

My fear and my powerlessness run together. As a child, I do not feel in control of my environment. I am still learning to master my physical reality. I meet new challenges with skepticism, if not with foreboding. I gradually learn that I am capable and move on to new challenges. Or I believe that I am not capable and my growth is arrested.

As an adult, I may attain some level of competence in dealing with the world, but my fear of new experiences remains. No matter how integrated my life seems, I inevitably find the boundaries of my psycho-social prowess. Perhaps I get sick, or someone close to me dies. I lose my adult face. My inner child arises with all his fears. My deep seated sense of inadequacy makes its appearance again.

Death is the ultimate event that I can't control. And so it becomes empowered, personified, endowed with intention. It becomes an assassin, an executioner.

Yet what if my metaphor for death were not one of punishment, but one of release? What if death meant a transition to a higher, less conditioned state? Then the fact that I die is not an indictment of me. Then I am not guilty. I have done nothing wrong. I have not failed in any way.

Then, I must confront my fears about myself head on. I must look on the painful images of self I have concocted, the unconscious shame. I must see that I caused my isolation. I chose to be separate.

My parents or husband or wife may have mistreated me, but they are not responsible for my feelings of isolation. Trying to make them responsible for how I feel about myself doesn't work. It means that I am dependent on their acceptance of me to come back into relationship with my self.

You see, that can't be true. That belief does not empower me. The opportunity to affirm myself is always available to me. No one can take it away from me. Moreover, the opportunity to join flows out of my simultaneous acceptance of myself and you. Only I can deny myself that opportunity to join by choosing to be separate.

All fear comes from the feeling of separation, and from the belief that it is possible to be separated from each other or from the Source of love. The fear of death, the fear of change, the fear of growth experiences that ask us to expand our boundaries, all stem from our belief in separation.

Separation is not real, yet I can make it seem real. I can stand apart from you.

If I stand apart from you, you will feel judged and you may stand apart from me. Sadly, this reinforces my sense of separation and tells me I was right to begin with.

Yet all this is a game of shadows. It has no reality except the one we give it.

We need to understand that we "fabricated" our sense of separateness through our stance/attitude toward one another. If we can change our stance/attitude, we can open the channel of love.

When I say "Thou" to you I ask to join. When I say "It," I back away from you in fear.

All my darkness comes from my belief that I am not "Thou," that I have never been "Thou" and that I will never be "Thou." This belief I project upon you. Thus, I always meet you with suspicion.

I cannot leave behind my inner darkness and move toward the light until I discover the "Thou" within. This is the task of self-forgiveness. And it is a lifelong piece of work.

Yet every time I say "Thou" to you, I lift some of the darkness from within, for as I see you, so do I see myself.

My shadow self is no different from yours. My shame is no different from yours. Oh yes, they have different sizes and shapes, but they retain the same existential address. They address us both as "It," for that is how they have been spoken to. And we speak back to them in kind. Thus, their shame deepens.

To redeem the inner child who hides in the shadows of fear and isolation, I must turn to him and call him "Thou." If I do not address him as "Thou," he will not respond to me as "Thou." I must rename him. In renaming him, I transform the way I perceive him. I remove the crown of thorns. And so he begins to emerge before me innocent and free. He gives back my humanity.

No, I have done nothing wrong. I merely stood apart from you and thought that separation real. Now, I see you did exactly the same thing. You judged yourself too. Now, there is nothing that stands between us. Now, there is nothing that keeps us apart.

❂

Part Two

The Practice of Equality

EQUALITY AS THE MEANS FOR JOINING

Joining happens when people begin to perceive a common purpose. Until then, separation rules.

Separation occurs when I believe that my needs are more important than yours, or your needs are more important than mine. All perceived inequality supports separation.

Separation leads automatically to manipulation and abuse. Distancing others enables me to treat them as objects. The more I address others as "It" instead of "Thou," the more I isolate myself, and I cut myself off from the love that I want. The exact same process happens if I allow others to manipulate me.

Now it is foolish to think that I do not have selfish thoughts. It is just as foolish to think that I should not have such thoughts. I am not "bad" because I perceive inequality. I am simply unhappy.

I see that my happiness comes in moments of joining, of perceived equality, when the channel of love is open. And I also see that my unhappiness comes in moments of separation, of perceived inequality, when you and I compete for love and acceptance.

I am happy when I know there is enough love to go around to meet your needs and mine. I am sad when I think that there is only limited love available. And I feel guilty when I receive that love and you don't, or resentful when you receive it and I don't.

This sounds very simple and childish. Yet all ego-dominated, selfish thinking and behavior comes from "children" whose needs for love and belonging have not been met. Of course, that means most of us.

Many of us did not learn how to go about meeting our needs in a healthy way. We learned how to manipulate or be manipulated, but we did not learn how to love and be loved. We did not learn how to accept and support each other unconditionally.

Our awareness of this fact is important. It gives us a choice.

I see that I have created my life out of a belief in separation by perceiving myself as unequal with others. That strategy has led to depression and despair. I do not lambaste myself because I have this awareness. I do not belittle myself and give away my power to choose. I simply see the results of the choice I have made. And I reject those results, along with the strategy that produced them.

I choose a different strategy, one that is based upon perceiving my equality with you, moment to moment. I choose to be aware of every thought of separation that arises in consciousness.

This is not because I wish to be a masochist, although, to be sure, when I bring my awareness to my thinking, it seems that the number of separation thoughts increases tenfold. Clearly, it is not the number of these thoughts that increases, but only my awareness of them. Still, this is the first test of my resolve to change my thinking.

At first, I did not look much at my darkness so I was only moderately miserable. Now that I am looking at my darkness, I am miserable all the time. Now I have the perfect opportunity to crucify myself, to be convinced that I am a good-for-nothing. I can leave it at this, which just makes it another exercise in reinforcing my guilt, or I can confront my darkness head on.

This means realizing that my self hatred comes not from my awareness of my mistakes, but from my judgment of them. My deep-seated belief is that the more mistakes I make, the more worthless I am.

So I add to my struggle with my ego, the ego's judgment of that struggle. Dark becomes double dark. Mistakes become self-condemnation. An opportunity to learn and grow becomes an opportunity to invalidate and tear down.

That is the test. Will I pass it? Will I walk through the fear? Will I look at the images of self condemnation as they arise and recognize that they are not me, but beliefs about myself?

All spiritual paths lead to the moment of self-confrontation. When I begin looking at my thoughts, I also see the emotional states my thoughts produce. It is not often a pretty site. But it is part of the process. It is the moment of testing and temptation.

If I allow these phantoms of consciousness to be real for me, I will have no choice but to turn away from them in fear, abandoning the very process which can release me. It is ironic, yet true. I must stand and watch the witches of my mind stir their brew.

Conscious awareness brings unconscious material forward. Fear-based beliefs and the emotional reactions that accompany them come crashing through when ego defenses are taken down. As a child, I learned to protect myself with these defenses. As an adult, I must come to realize that these rigid protective measures cut me off from the love I want and need.

When I look carefully at the tradeoffs, I realize they aren't worth it any more. I'm no longer willing to trade love for emotional safety. I need to learn to put these two back together. They were never mutually exclusive, except in my own mind.

This is what my healing process is all about: bringing wholeness back to a divided psyche. I don't want to spend my whole life defending against you because I am afraid of violation. Instead, I need to learn to be vulnerable again. Only then will I be open enough to receive the love that I deserve.

I may be walking with wounds, but you are not responsible for them. I am the one who has contorted and squeezed my body into the shape of my guilt. I am the one in pain. I am the one who is always pushing away, or the one who is always too needy.

Taking responsibility for our thoughts and their effects is not a safe, antiseptic kind of spirituality. It goes right to the quick. It raises our guilt so that we can see it and release it. It shows us the shape of our fears so that we can overcome them and leave them behind.

The world of separation is a temporary world of our own creation. Yet it will not disappear until we decide to let it go.

If we stand firm during our "forty days" in the wilderness, we will be able to say with Jesus "Get thee hence, Satan." For the only evil is the one we believe in, and that we must eschew before we can move from darkness to the light.

❁

A LITTLE WILLINGNESS

My innate goodness and yours are one and the same. That is the genius of creation. That is creation's equity and its compassion.

What I see reflects back to me who I think I am. If I see something negative, I claim that in myself. I cannot see something terrible in others that does not have its roots in my own mind.

If I see evil in others, I claim it. I think that by seeing it in them, I escape it. But it is the other way around. Whatever I try to escape through projection is subconsciously confirmed in me. That is the basis of guilt.

Guilt is the natural result of my judgment of others. It is a kind of cosmic boomerang. When negative situations arise in my life, I believe that I am being punished, because I perceive attack coming from others. But that is not the case. Others are just reflecting my own judgment or attack back to me. Whether we know it or not, we all are mirrors for each other.

What I see is what I get, because everything that comes to me will be perceived through my conceptual filters. I see an evil world and an evil world confronts me. I think that this is a demonstration of the reality of evil. It is not. It is a demonstration of the power of my own thinking.

When I begin to recognize that the way I see something determines what it means to me, I can experiment. I can have positive expectations of people. I can bless rather than judge and see what happens in my experience. If the law of mind is real, then positive thoughts and expectations will bring positive experiences. Like always attracts like.

If we choose to see darkness in ourselves and others, it will belong to us until we are ready to let it go. Extreme negativity palpably surrounds all who lack love for themselves. Such individuals are not ego-bound in the sense we are used to, but ego-injured. They feel a deep seated isolation and powerlessness for which they must compensate in some way.

Those who have been rejected and abused continue the cycle of violence. They live by the laws that they learn. It is too simple to dismiss such people as evil.

To say that there are some beings who cannot be redeemed is to reject the very concept of redemption. To be sure, there are people who do terrible things to themselves and others. Yet all those actions push them toward the moment of awakening, wherein self-hatred dissolves into the call for love.

Love is the answer for all of us. Each one of us has our bargain with the devil, our judgment and our guilt, for "which one of us will throw the first stone?" But this bargain is made in time, not in eternity. The devil is an angel after all. In this world he plays his role, as Judas played his, but in heaven he stands alongside the Father.

Is there a sin that cannot be forgiven? If there is, then atonement is impossible, and hell exists in heaven as much as it does here. As long as one man or woman is denied access to the circle, the circle is not complete.

As long as we do not come to recognize our equality with one another in the course of this journey in the body, we cannot enter the circle of salvation. Yet, we are not excluded. We exclude ourselves. As soon as we recognize our equality, we are welcomed in.

Our "little willingness" to change our beliefs, our conceptual filters, and our expectations of reality delivers us into the waiting hands of Spirit. By choosing what is for our highest good, we align ourselves with the law of love, and open the inner dialogue with God.

HEARING THE VOICE FOR GOD

It seems presumptuous perhaps that Spirit is available to me, yet careful consideration shows that Its presence is necessary if I am to surrender my fear-based patterns of interaction. I can be responsible for my thoughts, but I cannot know what greater good my thoughts serve. I may know what I need, but I do not know the form in which my needs will be addressed.

I admit that I may not perceive the truth in any given situation. I admit that the more emotionally invested I am in a certain outcome, the more likely it is that my perceptions of the situation will be distorted. So I learn to give the situation to Spirit and ask for the outcome that is best for all concerned.

I take responsibility for my thoughts and emotions, but beyond that I learn to let go. When my expectations are not met, I learn to see that perhaps they are inappropriate or too rigid, or perhaps my needs are being met in ways I cannot see. I do not judge the situation before me, because I truly understand that I am incapable of judging it.

Thus, my dialogue with God begins. By trusting Spirit I welcome it into my life and celebrate its guidance.

When my life gets difficult, I do not turn away from Spirit but reach out ever more urgently, for it is precisely when I am experiencing the greatest pain, that I am resisting the lesson I am ready to learn. And then, more than ever, I need to hear the gentle voice that brings me back to love and acceptance.

You don't have to "hear voices" to hear the

voice of Spirit. We all hear the voice of Spirit when something feels right and we do it, or when something feels wrong and we avoid it. Guidance is available to all of us all the time. The issue is not whether or not we hear our guidance, but how often we do.

If your intention is to surrender and be guided, you cannot fail to hear the voice of Spirit when it addresses you. Its guidance is often subtle and easily overwhelmed by the loud cries of the ego. But as you increasingly turn away from the ego's demands, the voice of Spirit becomes more audible and dependable.

This is a two-way process. Spirit does not move toward you unless you move toward it. It ever honors your will to decide what you want.

It is impossible to be a student of A COURSE IN MIRACLES and not develop an ongoing relationship with Spirit. The more the principles of The Course resonate in your mind, the more they come alive in your life.

You and I may read the same text, but our homework can be and often is quite different. Each person gets a unique version of The Course. Without the direct participation of Spirit in our lives, such uniquely designed curricula would not be possible.

So it is not presumptuous, but absolutely necessary to meet our teacher face to face in our lives. We do not study a mere book, but a living truth that transcends all differences of time or space. Because it transcends these differences, it can use them to address us in the form uniquely suited to us and at the time when we are most receptive to learn.

Whenever fear comes up in some situation and we ask for help, we will have some kind of demonstration of the presence of Spirit in our lives.

We do not need Spirit's help when we are effectively managing our affairs. We need Spirit's help when we feel out of control, when we are losing our peace, when we don't know how we can possibly go on by ourselves. That is when our call for love has its greatest intensity. And that is when the answer comes loudly and clearly.

A COURSE IN MIRACLES is an experiment in the dialogue with God through the Holy Spirit. It is not something we necessarily know how to do. It is something we learn through practice. The curriculum is not just what is written on the page, but what comes up in our lives as we are working with these concepts.

Each of us has a unique relationship with Spirit. It is not the difference in our experience that is important, but the similarity. The similarity of our experience is a powerful confirmation that the inner dialogue is happening in our lives and helping us restore our sense of joy and peace.

Our experience of Spirit is unique, but it is not exclusive. Everybody who wants to talk to God can do so. Anyone who thinks that only he can talk to God or that he talks to God better than others is listening to ego, not Spirit. The guidance of Spirit brings us together. It does not push us apart. It helps us realize our common purpose. It does not put anyone upon a pedestal.

❂

GUIDANCE AND ATONEMENT

The relationship between hearing our guidance and entering the Circle of Atonement is direct. Indeed, every time that we hear our guidance, we come to peace within, and this is a concrete experience of the atonement. Our guidance always reminds us of our sinlessness and that of our brothers and sisters. As such, it restores us to our consciousness of God's love for us.

To live in the consciousness of God's love for us is to experience the Atonement moment to moment. Only when I stop feeling loved do I stop feeling at peace. Every break in my feeling of peace is a break in my consciousness of God's love for me.

Peace is not something that comes and goes, although it seems to be that way. Peace dwells within me when I remember who I am and who you are. When my relationship with myself and with you is I to Thou, then peace is present in my heart. Only when I see myself or you as an object do I lose touch with my inner equanimity.

So it all comes down to my awareness of God's presence in my life. If I think that I know what is good for me, I may be right or wrong, but I do not invite Spirit to guide me. I invite Spirit only when I say: "I am not sure. Please show me what is best."

It is my stance that matters. When I act with integrity, I can be sure that I act with Spirit's blessing. When I'm not sure what course to take, let me pause and ask for guidance. Let me ask where I can find peace in this situation. This is a habit that must be cultivated. If I do not talk to God moment to moment as situations arise, how can I expect to hear the voice for God when I am distraught?

The inner dialogue is a constant reminder of my sinlessness and yours. It demonstrates that peace is possible here and now. It shows us in concrete ways that the grace of God is available to us.

EXPANDING THE CIRCLE

When I give love, I bring you into the circle of our innocence. Love is truly a gift because it does not belong to me. It is a state of consciousness I enter into when I see our equality.

Love is my gift to you, but also to me. When I choose anything other than love, I am isolated and alone. By seeking to ostracize you, I have chosen to isolate myself.

I cannot choose to love you without also loving myself, nor can I choose to love myself without loving you. This is not a truism, but a law of life.

What is commonly understood as self love is merely selfishness. My selfishness excludes you and isolates me. But real love for myself does not exclude you. It naturally reaches out to embrace you.

Love always makes love. It never makes war. If war is happening, if struggle and pain are happening, love has not entered yet. Selfishness has closed the door and locked love out. But love is always there, waiting in the wings. As the door of the heart opens, love greets us.

Until the laws of equality are understood and embraced, the concept of Atonement means nothing. There is no exclusive salvation in this world. What is true for some must be true for all.

Love is a continual choice in our experience because in every moment we decide whether to stand with others or to stand alone. To stand alone is different than to be alone. I can be alone with you. I can be alone with myself. In each of these cases, I am in relationship.

But when I choose to stand alone, I am choosing to be separate. This is an impossible choice. I cannot be separate. No one can "be" separate. I can only "be" in relation. The very word "being" suggests relationship.

Choosing to stand apart is choosing an illusion. It is choosing a world of "non-being." It is a perverse ontological choice, a kind of psychological suicide.

When I don't feel loved, I choose to be separate. Or to put it another way, separation occurs when I accept the idea "I am not loved."

The idea "I am not loved" prevents me from giving or receiving love. It shuts off my love supply, as long as I believe it. What we call ego is simply this belief and all the thoughts and actions that spring from it.

Ego wants love, but it will not ask for it. If offered love, it probably would reject it. Ego says: "Fine. If I can't have love, I'll do without it." Ego is the belief in love-deprivation and the defense built against love.

The belief "I am not loved" begins as a feeling "I do not feel loved." When I communicate this feeling, it is a call for love. I say: "I do not feel loved. Please love me."

To this point, ego still has no foothold. As long as I am either loving or calling for love, I am a being in relationship with other beings. I belong inside the Circle of Atonement.

Ego is established when I accept the idea "I am not loved." That idea is the basis of my shame. It quickly becomes "I do not deserve to be loved."

That is why it is so important that feelings be communicated. They are a bridge to the reality of inclusion. When I am able to tell you that I hurt, the hurt lessens. When you listen to how I feel, you bid me enter the circle of my innocence.

Feelings come and go. Sometimes I feel good. Sometimes I feel awful. This work is not about feeling good all the time, unless that is what is real for you. This work is about feeling whatever you are feeling without losing the awareness that you are loved.

So this moment may be a difficult one for me, but I remember that I am loved. "I remember that I am loved, but I don't feel loved right now." This is my call for love.

My call for love is honest and straightforward. It doesn't deny my feeling of disconnection, nor does it capitulate to it. It does not ask me to pretend to be "connected" when I don't feel that way, nor does it "feed" my feelings of separation with confirming thoughts and actions. It simply communicates how I feel. It enables me to ask for the love I think I lack.

Every time I ask for love, I connect directly with the Holy Spirit, whose purpose is to answer me. Spirit knows that my call for love is as close to love as I can come in this moment.

Spirit does not stand back in judgment and say: "How dare you ask for love? Don't you already know that you are perfect?" It simply answers my call for love with gentle reassurance.

So long as I do not fabricate my feeling of being unloved into a belief that I am unloved, I live under Spirit's guidance. However, as soon as I let that temporary feeling of separation become a belief about who I am and who you are, then ego establishes its foothold in my psyche.

Every day I have unhappy moments. Every day my brother or sister has unhappy moments. That is the warp and woof of life, the play of consciousness. The fact that I have unhappy moments is not a judgment of me. It is simply a sign that I am still learning.

Learning my lessons as they come up, however

difficult they may be, is still less difficult than pretending that I don't have to learn them. If I did not have lessons to learn, why would I choose to be in a classroom?

So I experience the highs and lows of emotion. That is just fine. That is the way it is here. When I experience the highs, I move upward without becoming inflated. And when I experience the lows, I move downward without allowing myself to get deflated. I take a deep breath and re-center. I am here. Up and down are just feelings that come and go. But I am here, in the center of my being: steady, on course.

Experiencing my feelings always takes me back into balance. I ride out the high and the lows.

It is a funny thing: experiencing my feelings enables me to let them go; denying them makes me hold onto them. When I hold onto them, I begin conceptualizing them, interpreting them. They become fixed beliefs about myself, rather than the dual play of emotion that they are.

Sometimes I feel loved. Sometimes I don't. When I feel loved, I am a channel for love. And when I don't feel love, I call out for it. That is the real rhythm of my life in this embodiment. Anything other than this is embellishment. Anything other than this is a belief in inequality, a belief that I'm special, that the highs are my special reward, or that the lows are my special punishment. This simply is not true. It is just my conceit.

❂

THE ILLUSION OF OUTER PERFECTION

I have a deep-set belief that my life will become perfect when I finally learn the right attitudes and behaviors. Until I overcome this belief, I will continue to judge myself unworthy. I will continue to carry my guilt around, interpreting every difficulty I experience as a judgment of me, or projecting that guilt and indicting you for my unhappiness.

My life is never going to be perfect in an outward sense. There will always be situations that test my patience and my faith. No matter how strong I am, no matter how deeply I listen to my guidance, there will always be times when I am overwhelmed and dysfunctional. To expect otherwise is to put unnecessary pressure on myself. To expect otherwise of you, is to give you a false burden to carry.

I am not perfect in this worldly sense, nor are you. The search for worldly perfection is a dead end.

If there is perfection, and I believe there is, it comes from the understanding that I am doing as well as I can. Sometimes it is hard for me and sometimes not. I need to accept all of the process, not part of it. Accepting all of the process helps release me from unnatural guilt.

It is not my fault that things do not always go as I would like them to go. It is not your fault either. It is just the way things are. Can I possibly judge what is and find it lacking? Do I have such certain sight that I can see what anything is for? I don't think so.

When I am in the place where life is not living up to my expectations, the only observation I can fairly make is that I am not being very loving to myself. That is where I begin to lose it: in my own consciousness. The outward situation can be a difficult one, but I am able to face it. I am not overwhelmed by anything external until I decide what it means to me.

Whenever I decide anything means something negative to me I am not loving myself. I'd like to put the blame for this on you, but that never lightens my load. It just increases my feeling of powerlessness.

The only thing that is true about this moment is that I am unhappy in it. The unhappiness belongs to me because I have allowed it. Let me not project the responsibility outward. Let me just sit with my unhappiness. Unhappiness is a fleeting emotion if I stay with it. Let me not try to make it right or wrong. Let me not judge how I feel. Let me just stay with it, be with it, listen to it. If I listen deeply I will hear it say "You are not being very loving to yourself now. Your expectations of yourself are much too rigid. Ease up. Be nice to yourself. All that is upsetting you now is not as important or as certain to continue as you think."

Let me not repress my feelings or justify them. Let me just be with them. They are an inner communication. They facilitate an inner psychological adjustment. That adjustment needs to be made. The feeling would not arise otherwise. Our outer lives are never perfect. Our inner lives are generally a struggle to release judgment or guilt and welcome love. That struggle is our journey, our life path.

We do not come here having finished the journey, but having just begun. Yet we all expect ourselves to be at a place on the journey we have not come to. We need to be patient. Let us abide where we are. Let us bring our attention to what is happening right now. Let us be where our lives naturally take us. That is our daily spiritual discipline.

We do not need special lessons, special practices, special teachers. We have all the spiritual challenge we need right now. If that were not the case, this experience would be an exercise in escape. True, we all try to take it in that direction, but it never works. We inevitably have to come back to here and now, to our specific lives, to this particular moment.

Coming home means learning to be where I am fully. As I find myself able to do this increasingly, the journey becomes less external. It is not about all the things I am going to do, all the places I am going to visit, or all the people I am going to meet. It is about what I am doing here with you. That's all that matters.

The recognition of my spiritual perfection comes through the acceptance of myself and my life. Of course, this does not mean that I stay in situations that are not good for me. I do not need to punish myself. I simply need to learn what sets me free.

Recognizing the perfection of my life requires an exquisite balance between learning my lessons when they confront me, and leaving them behind when I have learned them. I discover my perfection neither by avoiding the responsibilities of my life, nor by taking on inappropriate responsibilities.

Correctly seen, as I fulfill each authentic responsibility in my life, I move through a doorway of consciousness. If I take on an inappropriate responsibility, I cannot find that doorway, and I keep walking into walls trying to find it.

When I rise with courage to meet an authentic responsibility, even though fear rises within me and it appears that there is nowhere to go, I inevitably find a seam in the wall where a door opens. Spirit is always there to help when I am willing to take my share of responsibility.

Our journey has many challenges. We do not need to add the unnecessary burden of guilt to our task of forgiveness. Instead, we need to peel back each layer of guilt till we reach the essence of our sinlessness. We need to peel away all the unloving thoughts and feelings we have till we come to the thought and feeling that we are loved. That is how we discover who we really are and know that we are not separate from each other or from God.

ATTENDING TO THE PRESENT MOMENT

Let me be gentle with myself. Let me realize that I do not have all the answers and that I never will have all the answers. Let me realize that each moment of my life is an unfolding, an entry into the unknown.

Let me feel the newness, the awe of this moment, which has never been before and will never be again. In this very moment, I live and God lives in me. That is all I need to know. It is my ecstasy, my present happiness.

Beyond this, what can there be? Worry about the past or future is simply worry. And worry is always unnecessary. I can't change the past, even though I keep trying to do so. And I can't anticipate the future, even though I keep convincing myself that I can.

If I look without bias or sentiment, I will see the truth in this. All I can do about the past is forgive myself and you for the love we were unable to give. And all that I can do about the future is release my expectations, which limit it and hold it hostage to the past.

This is ongoing spiritual work. Again and again I ask myself: "who lives in me now, the voice of fear or the voice of love, the voice of judgment or the voice of blessing? Who lives in me now? Who thinks my thoughts and speaks my words?"

Spirit lives in me when I love or call for love. Without Spirit, I am a lump of clay. I am without energy, without vitality. Without Spirit, I am a mere form, subject to decay.

Without Spirit, I am ego's dark vision, self-created and self-destroyed. I exist only to judge, to attack, to kill or be killed. I am without meaning, without essence, an empty sack.

But because Spirit lives in me, I can climb from the pit of hell to the throne of heaven. Because Spirit lives in me, I live in its eternal embrace. My life is lived in its circle of grace and extends that circle breath by breath. Even when the body dies, that circle does not end, but opens wider to release me to a love that knows no boundaries or conditions.

In this moment, I am aware of my connection to God or I have forgotten it. Remembering sharpens my taste, my appreciation. Forgetting lets untold moments of beauty pass by.

A MIRROR

Every relationship I have had has been a mirror for me. With my friend the mirror was not that easy to look into. It took courage from both of us.

Here was this person whom I really loved and who really seemed to love me, and all of a sudden she was saying terrible things about me. She felt I was a fraud, that I wasn't the spiritual person I held myself out to be. She felt ripped off by me and she was full of rage. I knew that her rage was not my fault. In fact, I understood that I was innocent and so was she. But why was all this anger coming at me? What did I do to deserve it?

Our dispute surfaced around the issue of money, but it was clear it wasn't about money per se. Money was just a symbol of value. My friend didn't feel that I valued her. And I, in turn, didn't feel that she was fulfilling her commitments to me.

The truth of the situation was that the commitments I thought she made changed in the course of our interaction. We were both groping, feeling our way. When we were both trusting, the work flowed beautifully. When I worried about deadlines and she worried about being paid, there was a real struggle. Yet that struggle was not really about the work but about our attitudes toward that work.

When fear came up – and it came up from both of us – the work always got interrupted. I saw my friend's fear, but I didn't really have insight into my own.

Rather than confront this person about her inability to meet deadlines, I let the process go on. I didn't realize it then, but I was afraid to confront my sister. I didn't want to lose her friendship and I think

I really believed that she was the only person who could help me. The idea that other people could do what she was doing never really occurred to me.

By not confronting her, I maintained my friendship and kept the work alive, or so I thought. But, in truth, I did not honor myself or her. She began to feel pressured, resentful, and scared. When fear came up, it tapped into a lot of childhood tapes for her. So it was not surprising that what came at me was rage, not just anger.

For years I had hoped to connect with an artist with a spiritual perspective. Once that connection was made, I didn't want to let it go, regardless of the cost. So I held onto it, even when it was not working, for her or for me.

My friend had given me gentle hints that she might not be able to meet all of my needs, but I hadn't let them in. Even when she first blew up at me, I didn't understand that she was trying to communicate something to me. Instead, I judged the way she communicated. I didn't like her attack on me.

Of course, it was not the adult person attacking, but the child who had been abandoned by her parents and left to grow up alone. It was the child who loved her parents and did not understand why she was being left behind, or what she did to deserve abandonment. It was the child who was angry at not being heard or responded to.

While I was not responsible for all the charge behind my friend's attack, I clearly was the one who provoked it. I was not listening to her and honoring her needs. I was putting pressure on her. Even from a business standpoint, that pressure was not legitimate. I had a choice. I could have made a decision to work with someone else who could meet my deadlines.

The interesting dynamic was that I was holding onto this person and pushing her away at the same time. And she was doing the same to me. We were both playing out our childhood hurts and fears. For a while, each of us tried to make the other person into the bad guy. In her rage, my friend actually saw me as some kind of demonic influence in her life. And in my defensiveness over her attack on me, I saw my friend as an angry, out of control person trying to make me the scapegoat for all her problems.

My friend eventually finished the project she had been working on, but declined to go forward on other projects. I felt abandoned. Even though I knew that my needs were not being met, I was still attached to the idea that this was the only person who could meet them. At the time I did not appreciate what an outrageous predicament I was placing myself in.

Ironically, as soon as my friend made her decision, I began to meet new people who were able to help me with my work. I soon realized that this one individual was not the only "source," but one among many sources that are available to me at all times. Just because one person cannot meet my needs does not mean that others will not be able to do so.

My inner child of course did not believe that. Life had to teach him that lesson.

My inner child wanted to be loved unconditionally. He didn't want to be told one minute "I love you" and then the next moment pushed away. He wanted consistency, not emotional push-pull. "I love you, but won't you please go away" is a difficult message for any child to hear.

My way of dealing with push-pull was to withdraw emotionally. My friend did the same thing. It was our pattern. For years, both of us erected walls around our hearts and it wasn't easy for us to let others in. The fact that we let each other in was significant. And the fact that we re-experienced the old childhood "push-pull" in our relationship was not surprising. Both of us needed to learn that very difficult spiritual lesson that when you really love someone you not only let that person in, but you also let that person go.

That is a difficult thing for a hurt, love- starved child to do. First he doesn't want to trust you. And then, when he finally begins to trust you, he wants to make you the consistent, stable emotional source he always yearned for. He is looking for a mother, or a father, or both. He is not looking for a friend.

A friend says good luck when it's time for you to go. He blesses you. He does not feel abandoned when you leave. Somehow he knows that you will always be there in his heart.

We all have difficulty being friends, being equals, relating as mature adults rather than as hurt children. The more intimate we are with each other, the more difficult it is to respect and honor each other. The lines between adult and inner child become blurred. Old emotional needs and fears surface and become blended with present roles. The wife becomes mother, the husband father, or vice versa. When children come along, the whole scenario becomes more complex.

Relationships between family members and other primary partners are places where all kinds of wounds come up and need to be dealt with. They are places where "push-pull" is often the rule rather than the exception. They are places where subconscious emotional bargains are made and co-dependency is often the dominant shape that intimacy takes. It is difficult to get perspective on our lives while in the middle of these emotional dynamics.

Yet this is why we are here. We need to work through unfinished business. Indeed, every relationship which helps us bring awareness to previously buried aspects of our psyche brings with it an important spiritual gift. I see my relationship with my friend very much in this way.

I was given an opportunity to confront the part of me that continues to demand from others even when they have tried to tell me that they can't meet my needs. I got a chance to hear my child say "I have a right to have my needs met." And I also got a chance to hear the Holy Spirit's answer: "That's true, but you must let the person who can meet them come to you."

My friend was and is a gift from the Spirit, both for what she was able to help me with, and for what she was unable to help me with. In fact, I cannot now say which was more important. I suspect they are equally so.

I know that my sister received a gift as valuable as my own. She found out that it was important to trust herself, and to say no loudly and clearly when that was her conviction. She also found out that her rage resulted from a tendency to say yes when she didn't want to and then feel used in the bargain.

Yet what is most surprising about all of this is that my sister and I came together, not because we had different or even complementary lessons to learn, but because we had the same lesson. She acted out aspects of my inner child, and I acted out certain aspects of hers. We brought the darkness in each other to light. We were perfect mirrors for each other.

This interaction with my friend was one of the more difficult ones I have faced. I knew that we could find healing in it as long as both of us were willing to be vulnerable and willing to learn from it. As in any interaction involving judgment and blame, healing comes when both of us could be "right," and both of us "wrong." My friend and I both had to own our mistakes. We also had to own the legitimacy of our feelings.

We both had the right to make mistakes and learn from them. We both had the right to know what we need and ask for it. And we both had the responsibility to tell the truth, to communicate our thoughts and feelings, not as judgments, but as ways of honoring one another moment to moment.

I am grateful to my sister for helping me learn my lesson, for hanging in there with me when things really got tough. More than anything else, this interaction has helped me to realize that beneath all the garbage we are just two beings looking for love. Without each other, we might have had trouble finding it. But because of each other, we were able to overcome deep-seated feelings of separateness and discover ever more deeply that we are loved and blessed.

Part Three

Re-aligning With Nature

THE ENERGY IN THE HEART

Sometimes it can be very bleak outside. The clouds roll in from the west and sit over the mountains, resting there as they make their long journey eastward. As old clouds move out, new ones come in to take their place. Beneath the clouds, days are dark and listless. Faces are glum. Eyes lack brightness and the muscles of the jaw tighten. Joy, enthusiasm, indeed, energy of any kind seems far away.

In the late fall, after the leaves fall from the trees and the weather turns cold, this bleakness intensifies. The animals retreat deeper into the woods. People stay inside their houses more, going out only when they have to, bundled up against the cold wind that comes down from the mountains.

The whole earth seems in mourning. We get lethargic physically and depressed mentally. It is the first sign that winter has set in. You can see it in faces of people on the street. You can see it in your own face in the mirror. You can feel it inside.

The fire has died down. It burns dangerously low. Any moment it could go out, if the coals are not stirred.

In winter, the fire in the heart must be kept burning. We must take time to strengthen ourselves from within through meditation and positive thinking. We need to exercise physically and mentally. We need to bring up our energy, which begins to sink down as winter moves in.

In winter, there is a tendency to separate from one another, to stay in our own homes, in our isolated thoughts and worries. If we acquiesce, winter is doubly cold. We need our community, our sharing, our communication with one another to stir the coals. Intimacy gets the fire going again. Trust makes it burn bright.

When the fire of the heart burns bright, nothing from the outside can take its joy and enthusiasm away. It is not dependent on the weather or on the behavior of other human beings. It sings and lights the way from within.

Yet the inner fire needs to be cultivated. We must be sensitive to our energy levels, refusing to allow our vitality, faith and optimism to sink too low.

Winter is a time for real spiritual work, because most of the external reinforcements have been taken away. Upward and outward movements are more difficult, more intentional.

Inevitably, our awareness sinks within. We become more self-absorbed. If we have been running away from ourselves, this self absorption can be good. It can confront us with feelings we haven't made time to deal with till now.

A period of time for self communion is always helpful, but chronic self-absorption is not advantageous to our spiritual growth. It just brings our energy level down.

In the winter, we feel our biological fragility. We feel our mental/emotional instability. We have to work to maintain inner poise. We have to work to tend the fire within.

❂

WINTER AS A METAPHOR

Winter is nature's primary metaphor for the fall from grace. In the winter, we are furthest away from the source of light, so we need to make an effort to get every bit of light that is available to us. We need to rise earlier in the morning, take a walk when there is a break in the cloud cover, or just sit in the sun and absorb the rays.

Yet it is not just the outer light we require. In the winter, the inner light is even more important. Yet just as the outer light can be blocked by clouds, the inner light can be blocked by worry or fear. Whenever we entertain any negative belief about ourselves or each other, we invite the inner clouds to dominate our consciousness. In the winter, when outer light is scarce, we are more apt to be preoccupied with negative thoughts. Like it or not, our focus becomes more inward, and we are forced to deal with the contents of our consciousness.

That's why it is so important to bring our awareness to this low point in the yearly cycle. It is a time when we can make tremendous spiritual progress if we are ready to "go within" consciously.

Winter is the time when Christ was born. In a time of darkness and judgment, he showed us our innocence. He continued this teaching even on the cross. Easter, which is the symbol of the rebirth of life out of the darkness of winter, shows the triumph of Christ, the triumph of innocence over judgment. It symbolizes the reinstatement of grace.

Yet we do not have to wait for spring to experience grace. Christ was born at the darkest hour, in the depths of winter. We receive his promise at such times, when we are able to forgive the past and recognize our innocence. The moment of turning comes when we have completed the descent into the darkness of our own minds, when judgments are seen for what they are and let go at last. This is the meaning of the winter solstice. It is a time of energy transition, when the descent into darkness is complete and the ascent of light is about to begin.

The promise of Christ is the birth of innocence in our hearts. That birth is a virgin birth. In the midst of judgment, we find forgiveness. How it happens, we do not know. Suddenly, in the darkness, there is light. Now the days get longer and longer. Light has been reborn in us and around us.

Winter is the nadir of the solar cycle. There are other times in other cycles when energy is low and spiritual work is advantageous. In the lunar cycle, which deals with our emotions and our relationships with others, this happens just before and after the new moon. In the daily cycle, it happens just before and after midnight. These are all times when we need to center, let go of what worries us, and affirm ourselves existentially.

If we make a point of energizing ourselves at these low points, it will be easier for us to weather the psycho-physical cycles we experience. We will also become more conscious of these cycles and more attuned to them, resting and recharging when we need to so that we can interact and create when the energy cycle peaks.

It behooves every person who lives on this planet to come back into appropriate relationship with the cycles that govern its existence. It is impossible to abuse the earth when you are in tune with it. Only those who are out of tune with the earth are capable of taking from it without giving back.

Ecology movements are essential, but they must be more than intellectual positions supported from an armchair. We can't save the earth if we do not experience it. We can learn more from it than we can possibly teach each other about it. For ours is a head knowledge, not a heart knowledge. We tend to learn about the earth by studying it, not by being with it. That is why primitive peoples understand much more about the earth than we do. They know how to listen, how to cooperate with nature.

We need to re-learn that piece. We need to learn to be partners with nature and partners with each other. That means giving and receiving. That means understanding that what I give to you returns to me, and what I give to the earth also returns to me.

When we stop treating the earth as an object, as an "it," and start treating it as a "thou," our whole relationship to the planet will change. We will become listeners, enablers. We will facilitate the return to balance, outwardly and inwardly. For truly these two are related. Inner and outer environments go hand in hand. Each affects the other.

Re-cognizing our relationship with each other as equal sons and daughters of God brings us back to our charge as stewards of the earth. God gave us the earth, not so that we would dominate it and abuse it, but so that we could care for it as our home. We are still learning to do this. We are still wrestling with the same forces of greed and competition which earned us a one way ticket out of paradise.

If we want to re-enter the garden of Eden, we need to make peace with ourselves and with the earth. We are at a low point in the journey of this planet. And like all low points, this time requires an infusion of love, faith and confidence. Only positive thoughts and actions can heal the planet and ourselves. Only a willingness to listen and learn from nature can help us re-attune to her majestic ways.

LIVING WITH CYCLES

The phenomenal world is subject to cycles, to lows and highs, peaks and troughs. Highs are times when energy is strong and manifests outwardly with little resistance. These are times when plans can be put into action and the fruits of such action can be anticipated. Hard work will be rewarded. On the other hand, lows are times when energy is weak and turns inward, times when outward action is neither easy nor appropriate. These are times to let go of the struggle, to re-center, re-energize, and allow a new vision to dawn.

In between the lows and highs are points of relative balance between polarized forces. At the vernal equinox, for example, energy is ascending, building toward expression. At the autumnal equinox, energy is descending, consolidating gains and getting ready to let go of losses. Spring is a time of preparation when the fields are sown, and leaves begin to bud on the trees. Fall is a time of adjustment, when the harvest is brought in and the leaves begin to fall from the trees.

In the life cycle, the first twenty one years are a time of formation and growth. The next twenty one years until the age of 42 are a time of self expression and procreation, when careers and families are begun and maintained. The following twenty one years until the age of 63 are a time of psychological and physical adjustment, when children leave home and adults go through some form of mid-life crisis, often accompanied by menopause and related psycho-physical changes. The years from 63-84 are a time of retirement and spiritualization, in which the outward responsibilities of life are increasingly let go in favor of an inner focus in preparation for the transition out of the body.

Each one of us lives within many cycles simultaneously. Clearly, we all live within the larger cycle that begins with birth and ends with death. We also live within the yearly cycle that begins and ends at the winter solstice. In addition, we live within the lunar cycle that begins and ends with the new moon. And finally, we live within the daily cycle created by the earth's rotation on its axis, a cycle that begins and ends at midnight.

At certain times, several cycles may align. In some years, the new moon falls during or just after the winter solstice. Meditating at midnight during this time will help one get in touch with the new energies and directions which are possible in one's life. Such a meditation will be even more powerful if preceded by several days of spiritual retreat leading up to the new moon and the winter solstice.

Generally speaking, ideas and plans should be conceived and nurtured during the first phase of the cycle, and developed and implemented during the second phase. Results should be looked for and evaluated during the third phase of the cycle and adjustments made during the last phase, which should be a time of forgiveness and letting go.

The importance of the last phase should not be underestimated. No project ever turns out exactly as one expects that it will. Often, one has to change one's expectations to take advantage of positive results that may not have been anticipated. Moreover, the rebirth of vision cannot happen if one is emotionally attached to approaches that have proven ineffective.

When several cycles align in phase, it is always easier to accomplish the work which is characteristic of that phase. This alignment takes place once every month, when the monthly cycle aligns with the yearly cycle. For example, at the spring equinox, this alignment takes place at the first quarter of the moon at 6:00 AM. At the summer solstice, this alignment takes place at the full moon at noon. And at the autumnal equinox, this alignment takes place at the third quarter of the moon at 6 P.M. Each one of these times is like a guide post signaling the energy quality available and the type of work that prospers during this time.

Spiritually, alignment to the daily cycle is essential. This requires that we rise at dawn or shortly thereafter and get to work early, since the energy of the day peaks at noon. Early mornings are best for brainstorming and planning. Late mornings are best for tasks that require high energy or assertive action. Afternoons are best for meetings and cleaning up loose ends.

In winter, when there is less light available, the work day would ideally begin at 7:00 AM and end at 3:00 P.M. That would leave a couple of hours of light to unwind, exercise to release tension, and return home. Evening meetings or entertainment tend to interfere with this schedule and should be kept to a minimum during the winter. Afternoon and evening commitments can be extended in the summer when there are more hours of daylight available.

Alignment with the daily cycle will keep one's physical energies strong and vibrant. This will in turn help to keep one's mind alert and prevent unnecessary expenditure of energy in fruitless intellectual activities.

Alignment with the monthly cycle will help one stay centered emotionally. It will give one the energy to attract key people into one's life and it will tend to minimize inappropriate emotional attachments.

If you are looking to attract appropriate people in your life, hold your vision at the new moon, nurture it during the first quarter by being open to new people that you meet, increase your social activities during the second week, allowing yourself to take some risks and act intuitively on your attractions. Follow up new connections in the second and third quarter, but use the last quarter of the moon to spend time alone or with a close friend so that you can re-center, and re-affirm what you want.

Attunement to the seasonal cycle requires that new projects be conceived and nurtured in the winter, planned and developed in the spring, implemented in the summer, and completed and evaluated in the fall.

A more detailed description of the energy phases of cycles is portrayed in Chart One and Chart Two on pages 70 and 71. Chart One divides the cycle into four phases and Chart Two divides it into eight phases. Use whichever chart you find easiest to work with.

❂

CHART 1
4 Energy Phases of
Yearly, Monthly & Daily Cycles

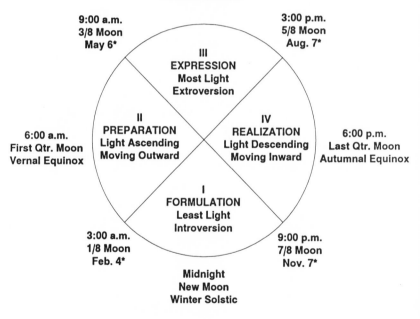

ZENITH

Noon
Full Moon
Summer Solstice

9:00 a.m.
3/8 Moon
May 6*

3:00 p.m.
5/8 Moon
Aug. 7*

III
EXPRESSION
Most Light
Extroversion

II
PREPARATION
Light Ascending
Moving Outward

IV
REALIZATION
Light Descending
Moving Inward

6:00 a.m.
First Qtr. Moon
Vernal Equinox

6:00 p.m.
Last Qtr. Moon
Autumnal Equinox

I
FORMULATION
Least Light
Introversion

3:00 a.m.
1/8 Moon
Feb. 4*

9:00 p.m.
7/8 Moon
Nov. 7*

Midnight
New Moon
Winter Solstic

NADIR

CHART 2
8 Energy Phases of
Yearly, Monthly & Daily Cycles

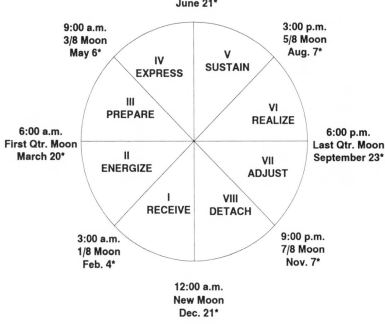

ZENITH

12:00 p.m.
Full Moon
June 21*

9:00 a.m.
3/8 Moon
May 6*

3:00 p.m.
5/8 Moon
Aug. 7*

IV
EXPRESS

V
SUSTAIN

III
PREPARE

VI
REALIZE

6:00 a.m.
First Qtr. Moon
March 20*

6:00 p.m.
Last Qtr. Moon
September 23*

II
ENERGIZE

VII
ADJUST

I
RECEIVE

VIII
DETACH

3:00 a.m.
1/8 Moon
Feb. 4*

9:00 p.m.
7/8 Moon
Nov. 7*

12:00 a.m.
New Moon
Dec. 21*

NADIR

*Note: Dates are for Calendar Year 1990 and may vary slightly for other calendar years.

INDIVIDUAL DIFFERENCES

The above information can be used by any individual to increase his or her sensitivity and attunement to cycles. Yet it must be understood that each person will respond somewhat differently to each cycle based on his or her temperament.

Temperament is shown by birth information. The day, month, and time of your birth indicate where you fall in the yearly, monthly and daily cycles.

People born with an emphasis on the first phase of the solar, lunar, and daily cycles, are idealists. They are good at brainstorming new approaches, some of which may be downright impractical. They do their best work in the first quarter of every cycle. People with a strong second phase emphasis can take an idea and develop it concretely; they are good at planning and preparation. They do their best work in the second quarter of every cycle. People born with a strong third phase emphasis excel at implementing the ideas and strategies of others. They do their best work during the third quarter of each cycle. And people born with a strong fourth phase emphasis are good at evaluating results and making helpful adjustments in the original concepts and strategies. They do their best work during the fourth quarter of each cycle.

Obviously, few of us are so easy to define. Most of us have a different phase emphasis in one or more of the three major cycles. This just reflects the complexity of our personalities.

Let's take a simple example. A person with a first phase emphasis in all three cycles would very likely be a visionary who tends to be isolated and has difficulty communicating his ideas to others. If we change just one phase emphasis — say that of the lunar cycle — to a third phase emphasis, this person will still be a visionary, but he will be more drawn to other people. As a result, he will probably make many strong friends and enemies, because his ideas are controversial. However, unlike the person in the first example, this person will be successful articulating his vision to others.

The season of birth is always the most important time of year for us. It is a time when we need to be in harmony with the sun's energy in order to be in touch with our ability to manifest that energy in our lives. If we begin to look at our lives cyclically, we will see how we receive opportunities to connect with our life purpose every year around the time of our birthday.

In a similar manner, the lunar birth phase is the most important time of month for us. Every month during this phase we are given opportunities to express ourselves emotionally in our interactions with other people. Being in touch with this time every month, helps us make important connections with key people who can help us carry out our purpose.

Finally, the time of our birth tells us what time of day is best suited for our spiritual practice. This is a time when we can benefit most from remembering who we are and getting in touch with our inner guidance.

It is not necessary to obsess on this information. It is meant to help you move with the flow of life, rather than against it. It is an important tool that can help you align your energies and movements with those of the earth, the moon, and the sun.

❂

BEYOND CYCLES

The study of cycles should not lead us to a mechanical understanding of the world we live in. If it does, then it does us a disservice. If we would benefit from this study, then it must help us to see our lives holistically and dynamically.

Wherever we fall in a cycle is perfect for us. If we lack a certain phase emphasis it is only so that we can learn from others who have that emphasis. Communication and cooperation are essential to our experience here.

The correct study of cycles does not make us jealous of the abilities and talents of others. It helps us recognize our interdependence and the beauty of all of our gifts. We do not look at cycles to divide life up into parts and categories that will help us define our lives intellectually. Quite the contrary. We look at cycles to attune to the rhythm of nature. Cycles repeat. Their repetition helps us become aware of them. We begin to notice how we feel during one phase or another. It is experiential. Without the experiential component, this inquiry is a waste of time.

Any person knows that his emotions go up and down. There are certain times when he feels stronger, more focused than others. If he knows that these times come on a regular basis, he can be prepared for them. He can plan activities at high energy times and times of rest and relaxation at low energy times.

Once we have attuned to a cycle, we no longer have to think about it. We simply start moving "in phase." Moving "in phase" means we honor ourselves and we cooperate with others. Unnecessary resistance, struggle and procrastination disappear from our lives. We are more relaxed and more directed at the same time.

Moving with cycles takes us beyond them. We no longer have to try to force square pegs into round holes. As a result, we have a lot more available energy to follow our guidance when it suggests a direction.

The concept of Atonement is not just about joining with God. It is about joining with each other, and with nature. We hasten the Atonement by using every opportunity given to us to expand our limited thinking. Thanks to cycles, these opportunities keep coming. If we do not awaken the first time, we can do so the next. The beauty of this universal Course we are taking, is that we keep getting the same lesson in various forms until we finally learn it.

In the end, every cycle brings us back to the Source of all, which is unchanging and eternal. It is that Reality which lies behind this one. And it is that Reality to which we attune as we move in phase with the Tao in our lives.

Part Four

Following Your Bliss

LOSSES AND GAINS

Ten years ago, I left the Northeast on a journey across country. My work life had been fairly stable for the six previous years and I enjoyed being financially secure. Still, I was not satisfied doing other people's work. I wanted to do my own work. I wanted to serve God with my genuine abilities and talents.

That year was a year of great growth for me. I traveled, went to workshops, tuned into my inner guidance, and wrote a book on divination which was to be published by a west coast publisher. The following year I got married and my wife and I had our first child. I wanted to continue writing, but my book had been put on hold and I didn't see how writing was going to bring in much income to the family. Instead, I decided to go into real estate.

Originally, I went into this new field with the idea of working part time so that I could bring in some money and still pursue my other interests. Unfortunately, I did not stick with my original plan. I saw that those who made money in real estate had to work very hard until they got established. I thought that if I was willing to work hard enough, I would be able to make enough money to live on for several years. Perhaps I would even be able to retire and write full time, I thought.

My hard work paid off and in three years I had started my own real estate company. I did well for the next two to three years. I bought a couple of investment properties and expanded my focus to include building houses and developing land. My goal was to make enough money to retire. For a while it seemed possible that I might be able to do it.

Then the market turned. Sales slowed down. I got stuck with a couple of houses with big mortgages that wouldn't sell. Instead of profits on my investments, I took heavy losses. My savings were wiped out. In the end, I came away with nothing, not even a house for my family.

After ten years of labor, I had less than I had at the beginning. My goose had been cooked.

Initially I resisted the decline in my fortunes. I schemed and I dreamed, trying to find some way out. But I inevitably ran into brick walls. I blamed myself. I blamed others. My accountant and attorney both said: "It's not your fault. If you had started this six months or a year earlier, you would have made a lot of money."

Gradually, I began to realize that I had been given a very powerful lesson, one that I would not be likely to forget. Instead of trusting myself and having faith that I could support myself by following my bliss, I traded that bliss for empty dreams. The lesson, put simply, is this: "if you aren't doing what you want to do now, you probably won't be doing it later." Or, to put it another way, "if you don't believe in yourself now, what makes you think you'll believe in yourself later?"

Putting off doing what I wanted to do gained me nothing, except about forty pounds! And a lot of bad habits. My attitude was more negative than it had been. I was more suspicious of other people's motives. And I was less willing to trust and open up to others. Being unhappy about myself, I had little love for others.

Curiously, as I watched things fall apart, I found myself becoming more open. I began to surrender to the process, and to feel elated as I saw old responsibilities drop away. My load was getting lighter. Now, I was only holding up half the world!

I began to turn within more and more for guidance. I reconnected strongly with my inner voice, which I had been ignoring. I began writing again. But this time it was different. Material just flowed through me from my inner voice. I didn't have to think about it. It just came and I wrote it down.

Several books followed. At first, I started looking for a publisher for my work. Then I got a very strong message that I was not to depend on anyone else to get my work out. I was to make a commitment to bringing my work out even if I had to publish it myself.

Once I made that commitment, I began meeting people who could help me fulfill it: artists, designers, typesetters, photographers and printers. Within a year from the date I made that commitment, I had five books out. I never really knew where the money was going to come from to print them. But I went ahead with faith, because that's all I had to work with.

To this day, I don't know where the money will come from to survive. Will I have the money for this book to be printed? I have to believe it will be there, but I couldn't tell you exactly when or how.

When I was in real estate, I was the one who was in charge. I made the money and I paid the bills. It was all very logical, while it lasted.

Now, I am no longer in charge. And if there is a logic in how money comes or goes, I do not know what it is. I work hard. I believe in myself and my work. I invest everything I have in myself and my work. But there are no guarantees of success.

My pay off is that I am doing what I want to be doing, and I am managing to survive. Since I spent a lot of years surviving without doing what I wanted to do, I prefer my new routine to the old one.

CLAIMING YOUR BLISS

"Following your bliss," as Joseph Campbell called it, conjures up images of people repeating mantras as they walk to their jobs at the local health food store making $5 per hour. But, if you think about it, it applies equally to people like Henry Ford or Martin Luther King, Jr., each of whom had a dream and believed in it.

We often hear the phrase "anything is possible." In my Book FROM EGO TO SELF I qualify it slightly by saying "Anything is possible if your desire for it is strong and it is in harmony with who you are."

You can't follow your bliss without strong desire. Often, following your bliss means going against the dominant assumptions of society. It means doing something that others can't envision or think can't be done. It means trusting the abilities within you that truly are unique.

You can't follow your bliss if you think you need to wait for someone else to give you permission to do so, or if you are waiting for the perfect situation or the perfect timing. Your joy does not wait for others; indeed, it rarely has anything to do with them, unless, of course, it is their joy too.

To follow your bliss and meet up with others who share what excites you, you must be willing to declare it, to proclaim it to the rooftops. You must have great confidence in yourself and enough chutzpah to be willing to make a fool of yourself.

The law of supply simply says that you get to do what you want to do most as long as:

1. you have fun doing it; and
2. others have fun when you do it.

It doesn't say you must believe in yourself, or that you must help others. The law of supply correctly assumes that you won't have any fun if you don't believe in yourself and trust others to receive as much as they can from you.

I left real estate when I finally realized that I was violating the law of supply. I didn't enjoy it. How can I possibly benefit myself or others from something I don't enjoy doing?

The protestant work ethic says that if I'm having fun, then I must not be working. It says that I won't find my proper place in life until I stop having fun and put my head to the wheel.

You don't have to be a protestant to subscribe, consciously or subconsciously, to the protestant work ethic. Few of us manage to free ourselves from its subconscious tug. Feeling guilty about enjoying yourself — whether in bed or at the office — seems to be part and parcel of the Judeo Christian tradition. Except occasionally in the arts and in some ecstatic spiritual traditions, joy is not valued in our culture. The assumption is that if you are joyous, you are selfish.

Most people view with skepticism the idea that you can be joyous in what you do and helpful to others at the same time. They don't even begin to understand the contention that unless you are joyous in giving of yourself you cannot be helpful to anyone else. Yet that is the truth.

NURTURING THE INNER VISION

As long as you are not following your bliss, you are cultivating its opposite: depression and power-lessness. Every time you turn down an opportunity to have fun or express yourself, you are robbing yourself of life energy. After enough refusals, joy seems inaccessible. Even when you look for it, you cannot find it.

If you spend your life doing what you do not want to do, you won't do what you want to do. This seems logical enough. Yet we don't believe it. We keep saying: "next year I'll do it." The longer we postpone our happiness, the harder it becomes to embrace it.

This doesn't mean that we should all immediately quit our jobs or leave our relationships. First we should concentrate on being happy about who we are and expressing ourselves. We can't allow our jobs or our relationships to so intimidate us that we are afraid to be ourselves.

When we have the confidence to be ourselves fully, inappropriate relationships and jobs simply fall away from us, like old skins we have outgrown. Appropriate jobs and relationships deepen and offer us new challenges and outlets for self expression.

Most of us are going to go through some kind of mid-life crisis. This is a time to take a look at our lives and see if we have done what we wanted to do. If the answer is no, we still have time to switch gears. Life is not over at forty. For some of us, it is just beginning.

There should be no sense of tragedy in the fact that it took us half of our lives to find out who we are and what we really care about. If there is a tragedy, it would be that we lived all of our lives without making either of these discoveries.

Authentic living is not possible without experiencing its opposite. I don't know what joy is until I have tasted sorrow. This is the reality of our dualistic world. I must first find out what I don't want before I can articulate to you what I do want.

The first half of life is all about learning what doesn't work for us. If we learn this, then we don't have to make the same mistakes twice. We can give ourselves and each other a second chance.

As Jung knew, in the second half of life, men become more feminine, and women become more masculine. The psychological balance shifts. That helps all of us become more complete.

After all, our journey is about wholeness. When we are fragmented, it is hard to feel whole. When we listen to the expectations of others, instead of listening to our own hearts, it is hard to feel intact.

As long as we are not taking responsibility for our own happiness, no one else will. Some of us have hoped in vain to find a relationship that would help us feel complete. Confronting the illusion in this isn't easy. But we must confront it.

If I am not willing to care for myself, nobody is going to care for me. If I am not willing to express my talents, no one is going to notice me. It is all up to me. Even when others begin to take notice, it is still up to me. I am always responsible for the life I create.

One of my clients had great difficulty finding out what he wanted to do in his life. When I asked him what he enjoyed, he could give two or three examples. But he didn't consider these things very important. He wasn't willing to step into his life and energize it. He wanted his life to come to him.

Unfortunately, this is not the way it works. You have to step into your life to get it moving. It doesn't matter if there is only one thing you enjoy doing; if you make a point of doing it, you will energize yourself. The more energy you have, the more opportunities you see.

Energy affects perception. The higher your energy level, the more optimistic you are. And the more optimistic you are, the more you see small openings. Small openings grow when you step inside them. Indeed, sometimes they become unbelievable channels. Yet, without energy, opportunities pass by. The options that exist are seen negatively and cast aside.

My client, like many other people I know, wanted his life all laid out for him. He wanted a roadmap and a guarantee. Yet even if he had these things, he probably would have had difficulty, because he did not trust himself and his own interests.

Faith in yourself is more important than knowing what you want to do. And knowing what you want to do is more important than knowing how you go about accomplishing it. Yet most of us approach career change by putting the cart before the horse.

We look at what other people are doing and try to pick something that is not abhorrent to us. And then we buy whatever training program promises to deliver us the job. We are primarily interested in job salaries, benefits, and retirement programs. The actual content of the job comes second. The idea of holding a vision of what we want to achieve in life is quite foreign to us. Some people would consider it preposterous.

Yet unless we have the vision, we will not have the energy to create. The fanciest "cart" in creation will not go anywhere if we do not have the horse to pull it with.

Our vision must energize us and it must honor us. It must be in harmony with who we are, reflecting our values and our deepest concerns. It must give us an opportunity to express our unique abilities. And it must challenge us by providing us with opportunities to grow.

Only when we have a vision that feels right will we find the energy to manifest it. These two go hand in hand.

A good horse will pull any kind of cart. The type of cart may flatter or offend our ego, but it is functionally irrelevant. As long as it does the job, it will do. Maybe we will trade up for a fancier cart when the time is right. But let's not worry about the year and model number of the cart we drive.

We cannot work with the energy of creation if we are always telling it precisely what we expect. The truth is that we don't know what is best. All we know is what seems to work now. The future is in God's hands. And better that it is in Her hands than in ours, believe me!

We need to be clear about what honors us and energizes us and leave the rest to the creative process, of which we are a part, but which we do not control, and should not control. Being clear about what concerns us gives appropriate direction to the creative process. The rest follows as a matter of course. We need not concern ourselves about it.

Living on faith does not mean that I do nothing. It means I do all that I can do appropriately. I speak for myself, not for others. I know that speaking truthfully for myself is all that I can do. Everything else must flow from that.

Yes, I must know my needs. I must tune into myself as deeply as possible. And I must have the courage and the conviction to say what I believe and what I want. But once I have done this, my responsibility ends. Then I must wait patiently for the universe to respond.

The universal answer to my living prayer is always appropriate to it. The form it takes may or may not resemble the form I anticipate. Yet the cart that follows the horse is the one that works best! Whether I am willing to work with it is up to me.

YOUR LIFE WORK

There is no prescription for finding your life work. The process is different for everyone.

You can't find a school that will teach you your life work. The only classroom that offers that instruction is the one inside your heart. Yet wherever people share from the deepest place within, that is where the work is forming.

We have institutionalized the learning process. We forget that it does not live in colleges and universities, but within our own consciousness. It has been the bias of society that schools prepare us for our life work. Yet that is true only to the extent that we have clarified our direction inwardly first and found useful techniques offered in the classroom.

If you don't know what you want, school is a terrible place to be, unless you are there just to explore, without career expectations. But if you know what you want, school can be a terrific place to be. And if it isn't, you won't waste your time hanging around just to pick up some credential.

Successful businesspeople know that a single handshake after an unexpected encounter can lead to a career opening that years of schooling would not have produced. Once you know the approximate destination, the process of finding your way emerges. Rarely is it a linear one. It twists and turns. Some of those twists are much more important in retrospect than the straight-aways.

The bridle path may be narrow, but it beats the interstate every time. On the highway, many connections are lost. The scenery is predictable and people tend to gather in the same place. In a crowd, there is more tension, unnecessary conformity and needless competition. It is an aimless place, an artificial place, a purposeless place. We only live in such a place because we feel trapped. But, sooner or later, we realize that we walked willingly into the trap. We finally understand that we are free to leave when we are ready.

I always say that if you are happy, fine. I salute you. If you aren't happy, then get off your duff and make the changes you need to honor yourself.

Every person on earth enters a wilderness at least once. That wilderness is the world of the Self. In it, each of us is tested. We are offered comforts and securities in exchange for our freedom. Often we take this test many times before we pass it.

All comforts and securities pass away. They are the moth-eaten and rusty treasures of which Jesus spoke. Only our freedom is eternal. And without this freedom, we cannot learn who we are or what our purpose is.

So if you find yourself in the wilderness, do not despair. It is but a sign of your growth, a sign that you are ready to let go of childish things. It is a sign that you are ready to take off your dark glasses and look unafraid into the mirror. It is a sign that you are ready to meet your brother and sister face to face.

Remember there are no guarantees or roadmaps in the wilderness. There is only you and what you know most deeply. Truth is your anchor. Joy is your guide. Trust in yourself and the universe is the path that leads from your heart to the heart of God. What other path can you follow?

Surely you will not take the one that leads back to enslavement and misery. You may retreat for a while, till you are ready to decide. But you will not go backwards, for you know now that the kingdom of

heaven awaits you. You have seen its majestic mountains and its deep blue streams. Like Moses, you have
seen the promised land. It matters not whether you
arrive in this life. Once you behold the land of milk
and honey, you will not rest until you arrive in its
midst.

THE LAW OF LOVE

Let's face it. We are playing now by different rules. The rules that pertain to the outer world are not the same as the ones that apply to the world within. When we give Caesar what is due him, we maintain our physical and emotional security and preserve the status quo. When we give God what is due him, we take risks which enable us to grow and express ourselves creatively and, by so doing, we inspire others to fulfill their potential.

The law of love, which is the only law God knows, is entirely positive. It does not condemn any being, but helps all beings awaken to their divinity. Those who live by this law often live unconventional lives and challenge the status quo. They do this not because they are revolutionaries or troublemakers, but because they are channels for love and forgiveness. They cannot help but witness for the truth that sets them free.

Every person we meet we greet with love or fear. When I look at you, I confirm your deepest guilt and shame, or I see you as innocent and free. Any gesture of love that I make is the essence of my vocation. My life work is to love, and so is yours. Only the forms of our work are different.

Any purpose apart from love is not God's purpose, nor can it truly be mine. If I would serve Caesar, let me be clear that it is him that I serve. If I would serve God, then I must be equally clear that it is God I serve, and then I will not be surprised that what God asks of me is not always easy for me to deliver.

For God challenges my ego and bids me face my fear. I don't have to be fearless or without ego. That in itself is an ego expectation, not a divine request. I simply need to be willing to see how my ego comes up without allowing it to take over. I simply need to recognize that I am afraid and begin to walk through my fear.

This is very important. It is an essential aspect of my partnership with God. My covenant with God is an agreement to turn to Her whenever fear comes up and ego asserts itself. Whenever I want to attack or defend, whenever I want to act impulsively or pull back from situations which challenge me, that is when I need to turn within and ask for understanding and strength.

It takes a while for me to learn to trust the divine helping hand. At first, I may be willing to do so only in low-risk situations. That is perfectly acceptable. Learning to trust the divine voice within myself is the first step in learning to live by the law of love.

Whenever I am upset and I ask "please help me find peace in this situation" and I find myself calm down, I have received the help I asked for. When I ask for peace, love, forgiveness, or understanding, my prayers are always answered, for these are spiritual gifts and they belong to me.

It may seem that I ask for help from without, but surely this is not so. The gift of forgiveness, the gift of love, the gift of peace, all these come from within. As soon as I ask for these, my ego-consciousness subsides, permitting a deeper connection to be made.

ACTING WITH INTEGRITY

Recently I applied for a job involving a fair amount of responsibility. I felt very ambivalent about the job, but I applied for it anyway. When I was called for an interview, I still felt ambivalent, but decided to go. Just before I walked into the room where the interview was held, I felt a lot of fear come up. What would I say to these people? I didn't really know why I was there. I wanted to turn around and go home, but it felt important that I cross over this barrier of fear. So I asked inwardly for help.

I was nervous at first in the interview but, in time, I began to relax and made some kind of personal connection with each person in the room. When the interview was over, I felt okay about it. I felt that I had shared some of myself and gotten to know the other people a little bit. I was more interested in the job than I was initially, because the people seemed genuine.

A few weeks later, I was called to come in for another interview. Once again fear came up and I struggled with it. My ego offered me a whole host of reasons why I should not go: the job would take time away from my writing; it would bring back old pressures which might set in motion old destructive patterns of coping; and so on. Surprisingly, my ego also offered me a host of reasons why I should go: I needed the money; it was a service oriented job and I would be helping people; and so forth. Clearly, my ego was in a bind. It wanted me to get cracking and bring some money in, but it was also afraid of the challenges the job would bring with it.

Then, a couple of days before the interview, I had a body work session with my friend Christopher.

During the session, I realized that whether or not I got the job was not the issue. The issue was that I have the courage to be myself either way. If I got the job I needed to use it as a vehicle for my self-expression and refuse to let it compromise my integrity. If I didn't get the job, I needed to continue my job search with the same integrity.

I determined to go to the interview and share even more of myself than I had the first time. After getting through the initial awkwardness, I was able to lay out some of my key beliefs and priorities as a person. I said that I didn't believe in top down approaches, that I was primarily a facilitator, one who sought to empower people to do for themselves. I knew that while they might find my beliefs interesting, those same beliefs might push them away from me toward the other candidate.

I really gave the whole situation to Spirit and said: if this is for my highest good and for the highest good of the agency, let this position come to me; if not, let it pass to someone better able to fulfill the responsibilities. I knew that, even if I did not get the job, going through the process was important.

By going through the process, I had a couple of significant opportunities to overcome my fear of exposure, a fear that has been with me since childhood. And the process helped me be clear that my only responsibility in any situation in my life is to be faithful to myself and honest with others.

Thus, the choice was not "to do or not to do," but merely to be. Being who I am may not seem like such great shakes, but it has been a life-long challenge for me. As a child I felt quite isolated and lacked confidence in myself. To this day, I am still afraid of situations in which I feel I have to perform for a group of strangers. Thus, for me, each time I stand up and say "this is who I am" before a group of people, it is an important achievement.

It is clear to me that God does not want me to stand in a corner. I am not useful to myself, to others, or to Him if I acquiesce to my fears and isolate myself. Thus, Spirit often provides me with challenging situations from which I can learn and grow. My greatest moments are when I am willing to acknowledge my fears and walk through them.

LIFESTORIES

I do not think my life story is that different from yours. Yet once I did. Once I thought I was the only one who had any debilitating fears. But I have learned that this is not true. My friends have helped me see that many of my fears are shared.

Occasionally I forget my equality with you, and fear comes up. If you see me ranting and raving, or running away from you at 90 miles per hour, you will know that I have forgotten:

1. that we are both afraid;
2. that we both feel unworthy;
3. that we both just need to learn to accept ourselves as we are, with all our fears and all our shame;
4. that our acceptance of ourselves and each other bridges the sense of separation we feel and opens the gates of love.

Yes, I forget that the only way to exorcise my fears is to face them. And I forget that when I face my fears, I make it easier for you to face yours.

You see, I have tried all my life to be perfect in my own eyes and I have always failed. It just isn't possible. The more I tried to be "great" the more horrible I felt. So I had to learn to just be "okay" in my own eyes. That was my first step in learning to love myself. "Ferrini," I used to say to myself, "you know, you're okay. You're not half bad."

When I could begin to do that, I could look at you with a little generosity too. After all, we're never harder on anyone else than we are on ourselves. We just don't realize how much we beat ourselves.

I feel that I am fairly knowledgeable about self-beating. It was something I did for many years without knowing it. It was an automatic process. I had to make it conscious. I had to see it and own it and turn it around. I could not begin to help you before I had done this for me.

Of course, this process isn't over for me. I practice loving myself every day, every hour, every minute. One minute I'm being nice to myself and, before you can say "frog," I've turned into one in my own eyes. It would be nice to put this behind me, but it's not so easy. This is a permanent part of my spiritual practice.

You see, I know now without a doubt that I cannot love you when I am not being loving to myself. This is true, not just as a general principle, but on a moment to moment basis. In the moment in which I feel I am okay, I am likely to feel that you are okay too. Even if you act inappropriately, I can see through it when I'm feeling good about myself.

And I also know that I cannot love God or commune with Her as long as I am feeling inadequate in any way. God addresses me only through my love for myself and my love for you. My love is Her channel. Without my love, there is no opening through which She can manifest. My love is the opening She is waiting for. Without my love, Hers remains unmanifest. With it, Hers pours forth with an intensity that is awesome.

So I do not have to hide my faults from God or from you. Spirit will take my faults, forgive them and use them to show me my innocence if I will let It. And if I am willing to be vulnerable before you, you will not strike out at me for my mistakes, but forgive me. For forgiveness is your nature. It brings peace to your heart and to mine.

The power of love cannot be expressed in

words. The whole universe abides with it and flows from it. It is the only law that brings increased freedom every time we submit to it. Love never enslaves us, but merely enlists our support.

The law of love functions only when we say yes to it. When we say no, it does not criticize or punish us. It just waits patiently till we are willing to receive its gifts.

When we welcome love, we see clearly that we are all in various stages of the journey home. No one is further ahead or further behind. Each person is exactly where he needs to be right now. And if that is true in this moment, then that is true for all time. In the openness of the circle lies its completion.

THE PATH OF EXPERIENCE

It may seem that the path of the heart is a dangerous one, but this is only true if we allow fear to block our way. Inevitably, fear makes its appearance when we are about to take a quantum leap in our growth.

When we are strong enough to break through old limitations, life always provides us with the opportunity. We must understand that these moments, which are often so difficult for us, come not as punishments, but as rewards for the inner work we have done.

No one is tested until he is strong enough to pass the test. That may not be the law in the classrooms of the world, but it is the law in the classrooms of Spirit.

The Jews believe that they are chosen by God and that is why they have had such a difficult time as a people. I believe this is true for every spiritual aspirant. Everyone who chooses God is chosen by Him.

Surely this does not mean that a vengeful God is looking over our shoulders, just waiting for us to make a mistake so that He can reprimand us. Rather, it means that everything that happens in our lives is a lesson in love and forgiveness. And when we ask Spirit to guide us, our lessons intensify.

If my lessons are blessings, then I submit to them. When hard times come, I do not run away like a boy about to be scolded, but I approach steadily, knowing that each test is a tribute to God's love for me. Just because God does not reward my ego does not mean that He does not love me. In fact, when my ego defenses come crashing down, then I am most intimate with Him, for then my heart is open.

It is often true that pain opens the heart. No, not the pain of torture, but the pain of loss. All love is of God, yet no personal love is the answer to our deepest needs. Only the love of God, which is unconditional and impersonal, meets our needs without deliberation.

Lovers come and go. Material possessions come and go. Fortunes are made and broken. Great romances burn with desire and then die out. All this is of God: both the giving and the taking away.

The role of Shiva, the Hindu God of destruction, is to take away our illusions. Ironically, this aspect of God, however frightening, is the most compassionate aspect, for only one who loves us most deeply can take away from us that to which we are overly attached. Such a God must listen to our cries of violation, our anger, and our shame. Such a God must love us so perfectly that he endures our fury as he leads us beyond desire and attachment to a deeper and wiser love.

No matter how much we resist, an essential aspect of the path of the heart is the stripping away of old beliefs and emotional attachments that prevent us from growing. These beliefs and attachments are developed out of resistance and fear. It is not surprising then, that when we are in the process of letting go of them, we re-experience the original fear behind them.

Experiencing that fear is never as devastating as we think it will be. This is because our defense mechanisms are not wrenched away from us while they still serve some purpose. Rather, as a snake discards an old skin, or a butterfly sheds its cocoon, so do we release the mechanisms of self-protection which we have outgrown. It is a natural process. It happens when we are ready.

To be sure, there is always some resistance to the process, and, as a result, some pain. But the pain is not unbearable, nor is it a punishment. Just as a woman in childbirth abides with the pain to give birth, so we too abide with the pain of loss as we are reborn in Spirit.

Pain never makes sense unless we understand where it comes from. When we know that pain comes from holding on, we can begin learning to let go. Of course, fear inevitably arises, but if we let it hold us back, the pain will just intensify. In the end, the only thing we can do with either fear or pain is walk through it. Resisting either one does not make it go away.

Experiencing fear and pain are inevitable as we follow the path of the heart. Ironically, the Way of the Heart does not take us away from our suffering but right through it. It is not a path of renunciation or avoidance, but a path of experience. Whatever comes up in life is grist for the mill.

This is not to say that suffering is valued. We are not encouraged to suffer, but neither are we encouraged to avoid suffering. We are asked to feel whatever we are feeling, and to experience whatever we are experiencing.

We must not exaggerate the pain nor minimize it. We must not run from it, nor hold onto it. We must be with it, and learn from it. Only by so doing can we leave it behind.

❂

THE ROLE OF COMMUNITY

It is difficult to follow the path of the heart alone. This way opens more profoundly within a community of witnesses. Such a community does not require more than a handful of committed members. They need not live together or even gather together more than once a week.

I have heard the statement made that study groups are not necessary for students of A COURSE IN MIRACLES. Perhaps this is so. Certainly learning takes place for all of us in every aspect of our lives. We do not need special times or places for our appointments with God.

But I do believe that support groups are very helpful to people who share a similar spiritual path. Personally, I have found a small community of people essential to my spiritual growth. Such a community functions as a place where forgiveness is practiced as a common goal. While the world at large does not support the law of love, the community of the faithful does. As a result, it is a place where intimacy and trust deepen, and we learn to give and receive unconditional love.

The community is also a microcosm of our experience. And just as ego arises in our worldly affairs, so it arises in the community, testing the spiritual practice of members and insuring that truth is lived emotionally as well as intellectually. This is the aspect of community life that gives us the most difficulty, yet it is also the aspect that results in our greatest growth.

Communities help to re-establish the extended family, which includes children and adults of all ages. Without the support of this larger social unit, many nuclear families will continue to self-destruct. Parents will suffer from economic pressure and children will be under-nurtured emotionally.

To survive with dignity on this planet, we need to rebuild tribal structures that emphasize fellowship among people, cooperation with the earth, and alignment with the law of love. As we grow in our individual journeys, we will begin to perceive common needs and goals that we can address together. Then, new social groupings will naturally emerge that meet our long-neglected needs for belonging and support.

Part Five

The Way of the Spiritual Warrior

SELF-CONFRONTATION

In spiritual terms, our greatest opponent is not an external one but an internal one. Our opponent is our limited thinking, our guilt, and our fear. Often, these are projected outward and we find ourselves face to face with someone who pushes all of our buttons.

Such meetings are difficult indeed. But we must not make the mistake of thinking that our challenge is an external one. In fact, no external conflict in our lives can be resolved until we find and address its cause within. We need to be thankful to those who oppose us in life. They help to bring our darkness to light.

Let us never dismiss an opponent as unworthy or undeserved. The fact that she stands before us is proof that we have met our match.

To run from such confrontations is cowardly. To seek to resolve them by intimidating our opponent is to forget why he or she is there. Neither force nor fear will help us triumph. For we are not asked to give up our rights, nor is our opponent.

My opponent stands before me because there is something we both need to hear. There is something we both are unaware of. My darkness affects him without my knowing it and his affects me. He stands against me, but he may not know why.

To be sure, the mechanism of projection is as automatic and precise as any biological fiat. I am always brought face to face with the person who shares my lesson and can help me learn it, as I can help her.

All conflict is a two-way street. There is never a right person and a wrong person. Each individual has his legitimate insights and his illusions. Unfortunately, they are often wed together. An opponent helps to focus the attention on the illusions that must be surrendered.

When each person surrenders her illusions, then the conflict is quickly resolved. Insights do not attack the other person, but help her grow and fulfill her potential. When it is fairly resolved, any good confrontation results in beneficial insights for both parties.

Each person emerges from the confrontation stripped of bias and misunderstanding and able to move forward authentically. This is the genius of conflict resolution; it does not compromise the parties, but guides each of them in a more appropriate and worthwhile direction.

It is a principle of The Atonement that each person has a unique and necessary role to play. The idea that one person's role can actually conflict with another's is misleading. For, truly there can be no genuine competition when every person has a legitimate contribution to make.

Of course, this is easy to forget. When I am not comfortable with my own role, I may try to compete for yours. I may even succeed in usurping your role. But if I do, I won't be happy in it. For I can only be happy doing what I love.

If I were already completely true to myself, you could do nothing else but salute me. How else do you greet someone who is completely intact? That is why, when two spiritual warriors meet, they bow to each other. They are like two old samurai masters who meet in the forest and bid each other good day. They know that, were they to fight, neither would win.

One never fights when the odds are completely equal. One only fights when one person believes himself to be stronger than his adversary. In the world, this belief is a common one. That is why there is so much fighting, so much unnecessary abuse.

But, in spiritual terms, this is impossible. All opponents are evenly matched. For each looks at the other person and sees her own strengths and weaknesses reflected. The deck is stacked against winning or losing. A different outcome is proposed.

AWAKENING JOY

As a follower of the path of heart, I realize that all suffering has its roots in consciousness. As such, suffering is the result of my interpretation of external events. By changing my interpretation, I can remove the conditions of my unhappiness.

In a deeper sense, my happiness is spontaneously present beneath my judgments of myself and others. It is not something I need "to create," but something I need to allow. Beneath and beyond all my interpretations of life, my heart is happy.

Cultivating this inner joy is as important as removing the barriers to it. Simple affirmative acts of being such as singing and dancing give joy an opportunity to express.

I had a tremendous experience of joy belonging to a group of people whose purpose was to love and support each other unconditionally. I didn't realize how negative my day to day life was until I experienced seven or eight people affirming me exactly as I was without conditions. And doing this in return for others was a tremendous privilege.

As joy awakens, it provides us with the creative energy we need to find our direction in life. To think that this direction can emerge without awakening our joy is foolish. Doing what we love to do is its own reward. As a result, we step into it fully, unconditionally. That gesture of trust and faith energizes us and gives our work sincerity and conviction. It is easy to build on this foundation, attracting others who share our enthusiasm.

Without joy, life barely has enough energy to sustain itself. Work is tedious and responsibilities feel unwieldy. Changing the external aspects of our lives is usually not the answer to our problems. In order to bring energy back into our lives, we need to learn to listen to our hearts. Energy comes from honoring ourselves, from doing what we enjoy and do well.

JOY AND FORGIVENESS

It is impossible to awaken joy without being willing to forgive ourselves for the mistakes of the past. New directions cannot emerge until we abandon old ones and stop punishing ourselves for perceived failures.

If you want to awaken joy, you must be able to start from a clean slate, as though the past did not exist. Actually it doesn't exist as a deterrent to your success except in your own mind.

Whatever your experience has been in the past is okay. It served a purpose in your life. You made mistakes and learned from them. If you learned from your mistakes, you don't have to repeat them.

Even if you keep attracting situations in which the same lesson appears over and over, there's still room for growth. Sometimes, the lesson may be a lot simpler and more generous than you expect it to be. If you have a habit of standing under volcanoes, the lesson may simply be that it's time to move away.

A recovering alcoholic knows that liquor makes him sick, so he stays away from it. A diabetic knows that too much sugar is not good for him and avoids it. And a person with high cholesterol knows to stay away from fatty foods.

We like to complicate life by making our lessons much more abstruse then they really are. In such cases, it is not the lesson, but our perception of the lesson that punishes us.

Much of self-forgiveness is commonsense: don't stand under a volcano if you are allergic to lava. This sounds facetious, yet much of our time and energy is spent battling in fights that are better left un-fought.

Guilt and lack of common sense go hand in hand. They both are energy wasters.

A spiritual warrior must conserve his energy. If he spends all of his time fighting windmills like Don Quixote, he will have little energy left to do battle with legitimate opponents. We have to face our fears or we will not overcome them. That is true. When the fight comes to us, we must learn to stand our ground. But we should not go out looking for a fight. If we do, we are likely to find it and jeopardize our strength.

It is easier to become overburdened than it is to lay our burdens down. It is easier to become overextended than it is to regain our strength. We all have to learn this.

I am here to carry myself, not to carry others or be carried by them. This does not mean that I decline to help when the opportunity arises or that I decline assistance when I need it. It simply means that I take appropriate responsibility for my life. I try not to be in the role of helper or helpee all the time. The more I change roles, the less chance I take that I will become attached to the role I play.

So, the spiritual warrior can be very strong and forthright. And she can also be very gentle and diplomatic. It depends on the situation and her ability to respond effectively to it.

A spiritual warrior never makes a show of strength unless it is necessary. He keeps his strength hidden within, where he can nurture it. He knows his greatest challenge is mastering his own fear. If he can do that consistently, there is no external opponent or situation that can defeat him.

❁

NON-FORCING

The Taoists accurately see life as a flow that is enjoyed most when one moves with it rather than against it. Any time we have to force something to happen in our lives, we are violating the Tao, or the way of life. This brings difficulty for ourselves and others.

For example, a small stream can be easily diverted to make a pond, but the waters of a large river cannot so easily be contained. It will take a great effort to accomplish.

If energy or ability is not great, only small efforts should be undertaken. After many successful smaller efforts, energy and skill are developed and more demanding efforts can be considered.

Moving with the Tao means developing an inner sense of what is appropriate in each situation. I recently received an important lesson on this subject.

When I was a child, I studied the trumpet. I worked hard at it and was getting pretty good when all of a sudden my embouchure collapsed. I couldn't hit the high notes any more. In panic, I went to a specialist who played first chair trumpet for a symphony orchestra. He took one look at the way I played and said: "You learned your embouchure incorrectly. You place the mouthpiece up against the fleshy part of your upper lip. Those muscles are not strong and they have collapsed under the strain. The correct way to play is to roll your upper lip so the mouthpiece rests on the top. That's not going to be easy for you to relearn, because every time you put the mouthpiece to your lips you are going to want to place it the way you are used to. When you place it correctly, you won't sound good at all. It will be very frustrating to you, like starting from scratch. In fact, I think you would find it easier to take up a new instrument. If I was you, that's what I would do."

I was devastated. I tried for a while to relearn, but I just couldn't accept how badly I sounded. Finally, I quit entirely.

After five years of living without music, I learned to play the flute. This brought me great enjoyment, particularly when I began playing classical duets with my friend Debbie. Unlike the trumpet, playing the flute requires a very open and relaxed embouchure. Although I did not know it at the time, it was a perfect choice for me.

Recently I was in a music store, waiting for my son to finish his clarinet lesson, when I spotted a nice looking trumpet in the glass case. "Do you mind if I try that trumpet," I asked the owner. "Help yourself," he said.

I played the trumpet with great difficulty, but I didn't seem to be placing the mouthpiece incorrectly, as I had before. I decided to take the instrument home and try it for a month.

For the first few days, I attacked the instrument, trying to hit as many notes as I could. I was somewhat encouraged, but my lips tired greatly after playing for ten or fifteen minutes. And, even though I could hit a few high notes, I could not sustain them. I decided to have a lesson to make sure my embouchure was correct.

The lesson was a revelation to me. My teacher asked me to play softly, and I couldn't. I couldn't even hit the lower notes without playing loudly. Then he gave me a series of simple exercises, playing long tones as soft as possible. He said not to worry whether or not I hit the right notes, but just to play softly and sustain whatever sound came out of the instrument.

I tried this for several minutes. I sounded absolutely terrible, but there was no forcing in my playing. My lips were reasonably relaxed and I was not tired after playing the exercise.

Suddenly, something clicked inside of me. I understood why I would never learn the instrument as long as I tried to push myself beyond my present ability. The only way I would be able to learn was if I accepted where I was and learned to play in a more relaxed way.

I understood that it was not only my embouchure that had been incorrect when I had played before. My attitude toward playing was also incorrect. I had not been taught to relax and take small steady steps.

So now, after a detour of almost thirty years, I find myself returning to the instrument of my youth with an appropriate attitude. Maybe now, if I really want to, I can learn to play.

To me, my trumpet story isn't just an amusing anecdote, but an important illustration of the concept of "non-forcing." When I accept myself as I am and do not put artificial pressure on myself to succeed, I am able to develop my abilities in a natural way. While the natural way does not often bring the short term results that come from pushing, it does bring the only long term success.

As a man, my best sexual experiences have been when I have been completely relaxed and trusting of myself and my partner. My worst experiences have come when I have had a lot of expectations of myself or of her. Indeed, force of any kind, whether physical or psychological, is completely inconsistent with making love.

No physical action achieves its full potential unless there is an element of relaxation present in it. And relaxation begins in the mind. It is an approach of peace, instead of struggle. It is a movement that flows out from an inner stillness.

Activity and rest go hand in hand. You cannot have one without the other. As in all things, balance is to be sought. Balanced people know when to stand up for themselves, and when to defer to others. They do not allow their rights to be compromised, nor do they impose their will on others. Because they are balanced within, they find equality without. That is the secret. That is the Tao.

The spiritual warrior listens to the Tao and learns from it. Feeling safe, he offers safety to others. Resting in the heart, he bids others return home.

TOO LITTLE AND TOO MUCH

In my Book *VIRTUES OF THE WAY*, the voice of Spirit says:

> *Do not say it is too little.*
> *Do not say it is too much.*
> *Simply receive*
> *What I give in each moment.*

If I think what I receive is too little, then I probably don't value what I have. If I think it is too much, then I have the same lesson, but my process of learning it will be different. If I keep getting the message "too little," I must start valuing myself more energetically. It is time to stand up and be counted. It is time to give, to participate, to make my contribution to life, however small.

If I keep getting the message "too much," it is time to receive what life offers me without guilt or resistance. Let me welcome the gift that comes from others or I won't be able to offer it back to them when it is time.

In reality, nothing is too little or too much. We just have the perception that it is. That perception says more about us than it does about external factors.

Whatever is given to us is enough if we truly receive it. And whatever we have to give is enough if we are not afraid to give it. Our problem is not one of supply.

Our problem is one of gratitude and trust. We do not value what we have. We do not celebrate it and give thanks for it. We experience a "lack" in what we have. And so we look to be supplied from without. We look to be supplied in the future. This is not empowering here and now.

On the other hand, when we are grateful for what we have, we experience it as abundant. Even a little bit of something seems like a lot. And because we feel fulfilled by it, we are more willing to share it. Our gratitude enables us to trust our supply and act with energy and faith. It is precisely this energy, faith, and consciousness of supply that Jesus was in touch with when he was able to feed the multitude of 5,000 people with five loaves of bread and two fishes.

A COURSE IN MIRACLES teaches us that there is no order of difficulty in miracles. Feeding five thousand people is no more difficult than feeding one person if we are in touch with the Source of our supply.

Clearly, we cannot be in touch with that Source if we find the present circumstances of our lives wanting. We must build on what we have, not on what we do not have.

We all have something. It may not be very much, but if we believe in it and use it confidently, we will add to it. We increase our physical supply by being aware of it here and now. This is not a magic formula. It works only if we enter into it wholeheartedly.

All through our lives we are faced with the question: "Do we have enough?" Those who say "no" embark on a futile search for that which they think is missing from their lives. It might be a job, a relationship, a house, a bank account, or even a spiritual experience. They will return older and wiser.

It is clear that the greatest obstacle to our inner peace and abundance is that we resist or simply don't value what we have. How can we be happy if we think we don't have what we need? It isn't possible.

The search for "more" or "better" has no end. Once we find what we think we want, there will always be "more" of it to find. Then there will be more anxiety, more planning, more disruption of our lives.

Only when we say that what we have is "enough"

are we able to enjoy this moment. That is when we begin to feel peaceful. That is when we begin to notice the little things of beauty in our lives.

Peace is not something that can be found through striving. Abundance is not something we have to earn. Peace flows from the simple act of being who we are. Abundance flows from the simple enjoyment of and gratitude for what we have.

THE BELOVED

We seek the Beloved, but we do not know who she is. She takes the shape of our hopes, our desires, sometimes even our fears. We seek the Beloved, but when she comes to us, we do not notice her. And when we try to get close to her, she slips away from us.

Who is the Beloved?

Quixote had his Dulcinea. Without her, he would not have been inspired to don his armor, mount his steed, and go off in search of adventure.

We all have our Dulcinea, whom we seek to honor and please, though often she does not know that we exist. And even if we do not have a muse in the flesh, we seek to honor some lofty ideal. We all live for some goal we aspire to achieve.

That is par for the course. The spiritual warrior goes off in search of enlightenment and comes back softened and mellowed by the journey. Perhaps he did not find what he set out to find. But what he found was valuable nonetheless. If asked, he would not trade it, even for the elusive embrace of his muse.

We all have our muses, yet each is just the superficial face of the Beloved. The muse knows us casually and cannot understand our devotion, but the Beloved knows us well. Her dance is an elusive one, taking us in and out of many embraces.

Too little desire will not attract her. Yet too much desire drives her away. We are ever trying to find the right balance to bring her to us and encourage her to stay.

Thinking she expects us to be self-reliant, we look for her within, only to find her looking back at us through the faces of people we have taken for granted. Thinking that she wants us to be practical, we look for her in the faces of our intimate friends, only to see that she has once again made her home within.

As long as we need her, she remains aloof. Only when we are ready to give her up forever does she consent to be with us. She is the one who draws us out and draws us in, a master teacher to be sure. When we finally arrive in her presence, there is no territory of heart or mind we have not traversed. There is no bondage we have not suffered, no freedom we have not gained.

In the end, she rests with us, in the peace of our hearts. She is quiet now, a silent companion, a sister and a friend. There is no desire that separates us, no fear that keeps us apart.

THE CIRCLE OF JOINING

The spiritual path is a circular one, not a linear one. It does not take you away from where you are, although it may sometimes appear to. In the end, the circular path always brings you home.

Consciousness of self requires differentiation from others. The small child becomes aware of herself as she detaches from her mother and begins to direct her own life. This "ownership" of her life is an essential developmental phase. It enables her to build a self-concept and take responsibility for the choices she makes.

In time she becomes involved with other men and women and her self-concept is tested and refined. When she becomes a mother, her sense of self expands to make room for her bonding with her children. That joining is so intense, it becomes a metaphor for her relationship with all of life.

Her experience of differentiation was temporary and served a purpose. In the same manner, her experience of joining with her children serves its rightful purpose, expanding her social boundaries and bringing her into closer relationship with others in her community.

As her children grow and embark on their own journey to independence, she must learn to let them go. Thus, she comes full circle. Now, it is time for her to bring the outward and inward aspects of the journey together inside herself.

Now she is alone, but not separate from others. Joining has become a conscious process. She meets others not as "daughter" or as "mother," but as equal. She needs both to give and receive.

Her awakened sense of self gives her the confidence and the courage to meet others authentically. And her awareness of that flowering of self in others helps her respect who they are and honor their needs. Thus, she begins to be aware of her relationship to the divine within herself and others. Not that she was unaware of this before, but now she has the time and interest to explore her spirituality more fully.

As intimacy increasingly becomes a conscious proposition, old boundaries fall away, and she is able to be close to more and more people. The circle of grace widens in her life. Intuition plays a greater role. And the line between ego and Spirit begins to disappear.

What is God and not God? It is not so easy for her to say. Moral absolutes are inaccurate and no longer comforting. People around her complete their journeys in the body, and she begins to realize that hers too will soon be over.

God is no longer an abstraction, but a living presence in her life. All that once seemed separate begins to seem less distinct. Preferences begin to fade away. Now there is just a gentle appreciation of life as it unfolds in each moment.

Time slows down. Memories from the past return. They no longer seem so distant. The line between past and present melts away. The eyes look more within. There are worlds there that need to be explored.

The journey between life and death is no longer a linear one. She is returning to the place of her birth, to the moment just before the first sense of separation was felt. When she arrives there, she will no longer be in the body. Her peace will no longer come and go. It will be eternal.

We all take this journey to and from our Source. In it we experience separateness and joining. As we become increasingly conscious of who we are, we begin to realize that we are unhappy in our sense of separateness. To be sure, it is important that we develop our uniqueness, but we need to do it in a way that makes us feel connected with others.

Honoring ourselves may seem to set us apart, but it does not do so without our permission. If we are willing to open our hearts, we can be ourselves and feel connected to others. And if we overcome our co-dependency, we can be intimate with others without losing our sense of self.

The I Ching says that one must know when to separate and when to unite. Truly, a balance must be found between honoring ourselves and honoring others, between being apart and being together. True intimacy knows no separation of time or space. It is sustained and deepened by the authentic development of each being.

These are the simple but profound lessons we are here to learn. Our journey in the body — whether it happens once or many times is not significant — enables us to learn these lessons as often as we need to.

Knowing that I am I is one movement. Knowing that I am you and you are me is another. Knowing that I am God and God is me is the last awareness, the one which Jesus taught.

This is the holy trinity and we must understand it fully before we can take our rightful place in it. Till then, the circle of joining welcomes us in every moment.

Yes, we will forget, and then remember. Let there be no blame in this. We will separate and unite. We will venture forth and return home. This happens every moment. The whole journey is present now. All of it is right here right now.

THE HOLY INSTANT

It is an absolutely remarkable thing that as long as I stay in this moment, I am happy. Even if I think I am unhappy, if I stay with my unhappiness, I can find the place where it ends and joy begins.

Past and future make the cross of my suffering. I can carry it or put it down. To be sure, if I choose to carry it, I will be crucified upon it.

Only in this moment am I whole and free. In this very moment is the circle of grace around me. At-one-ment begins here and now. Let me not place it in the future, or I shall not find it.

If we are joined deep within, beneath the temporary illusion of Separation, as A COURSE IN MIR-ACLES teaches us, then there is nothing that we need to do or say to experience our intimacy. It is simply there. We can welcome it or place expectations around it.

Every expectation I have of you or me takes me out of the present moment. Let me say that again. Every expectation I have of you or me takes me out of the present moment. Every expectation I have stands between my present love and acceptance of myself and my present love and acceptance of you.

The spiritual warrior faces facts. The way is not hard to understand, but it is hard to practice. Most of our time, we argue about which direction to take. But that isn't the issue at all. The issue is practicing what we know right now. The way opens to the practice of it.

Prayer means nothing without practice. If I call out for guidance, I need to listen to and follow through with that guidance. Otherwise, I will keep calling out in vain for help. That's not because God doesn't answer me, but because I'm not hearing the answer, or, if I am, I'm not putting it to work in my life.

Following our guidance is scary. There's no question about that. It usually goes against everything we think we should do. That's because the answer to the problem comes from a higher level than the problem, and on that level the problem does not exist.

From a distance, the rope looks like a snake and inspires fear. I don't want to approach, yet my guidance says "full speed ahead." With great trepidation I move forward. When I get close to the rope, I see that it isn't a snake and my fear subsides.

Do you know how many times I see snakes where there are none? Do you know how many times fear comes up for me when there is nothing to be afraid of?

Spiritual practice means staying in the present and facing our fears. That is the warrior's path. It is not complicated, but few of us stay on it. Detours appear in the guise of short-cuts. We branch out, getting lost in the woods, or go out on a limb only to get terrified looking down. Meanwhile, the footpath winds slowly up the mountain.

That's okay. No need to rush. It seems that we have lost time, but remember, this isn't a race. It doesn't matter when you get there. It may not even matter if you get there at all. Perhaps you are already there and just don't know it. How Can you say?

You can't. You can only focus on what's before you. If you get side-tracked, come back. If the path turns sharply up hill, take your time. You have all the time you need to finish your journey.

Many of us fear the end of the world. We think

we're running out of time. That is the methodology of guilt. Don't subscribe to it. You have done nothing you need to be punished for.

If you would do something for your brother or something for the earth, do it now. Tomorrow does not exist except in your own mind. And all it holds are grim images of death. Let them die upon the cross without your help.

You are needed here, not there.

This moment is an invitation to love and overcome fear. That is all it ever was and all it ever will be. Things seem to change, to move ahead or behind, but it is not so. The only thing that changes is your answer to the invitation.

Come home, gentle friend, not in some distant future, where we met once or will meet again, but right now. If I am here, you cannot be very far away.

❂

Part Six

Dancing in the Mirror

IS GOD DEAD OR ALIVE?

Growing up in an atheist family, the only time I really thought about God was when someone died. My parents didn't believe in telling me sugar coated stories, so I never got the consoling thought "It's okay, grandpa is in heaven;" or "he's with God now." In my world, there was nothing benign about death. And if there was a God, I speculated, there was nothing benign about Him either.

I was particularly devastated when my cousin Deirdre died. I was thirteen and Deirdre was fifteen. She was my favorite cousin. She had a certain beauty and innocence. I loved being with her. When she got sick, I was told she had anemia and that, if she took iron pills, she'd get better. A couple of days after that she died from Leukemia.

She was swept away without rhyme or reason. I was in shock. I had never really talked to God before, but now I talked to Him every night through my tears. You see, I had been wounded. Someone I loved had been taken from me and I didn't understand. I asked God why? I got no answer. I tried to bargain with Him: "You can have me instead; just bring Deirdre back," but apparently He did not make deals.

In my perception, God was at best uncaring, if not actually cruel. I needed a spiritual perspective to bring me some comfort, to introduce something positive in this experience, but my parents had none to offer. Or if they did, they kept it to themselves. I was left alone with this death.

At thirteen, my approach to God was defensive. I was hurt and outraged. I came to God empty handed. I had no faith. I demanded an answer and I received stone-cold silence.

I did better as an adult, ten years later. I can't

really tell you why. Perhaps it was because it was my own life that was on the line then. And I really did ask for help. Surprisingly, help came. I was given a lifeline.

I heard the tiniest of voices inside. It was so small, it would have been easy to ignore, had I not been listening intently. Fortunately for me, I decided to listen to it.

Still, the idea of being able to communicate somehow with God through my own mind seemed foreign to me. It took many years for me to realize that it was an ongoing possibility.

One test of faith came when I was in tremendous grief over the break up of a relationship. Linda and I were planning to have a child together and she left not long after she had gotten pregnant. I felt doubly wounded. I was not only losing the woman who had told me she loved me, but the child we had conceived together in love. I remember rolling around on the floor sobbing. I ached deep down inside. I just couldn't handle the pain alone. Again, I asked for help.

I meditated for about a half an hour, gradually rising through my pain into a calm space, in which I heard a gentle voice re-assuring me. "You are all right," said the inner voice. "You didn't do anything wrong. She just got scared and ran away. It's not your fault. Just because she left does not mean you are not worthy of love. You are! But you can't hold onto Linda. You need to love and care for yourself."

These words comforted me and helped me get through a difficult night. They did not make my grief go away. It took over a year for that to happen. But, whenever I turned within for guidance and strength, I was addressed with love and understanding. I was comforted, as a child is comforted by his parents when he gets hurt and does not understand why.

Each of us has a spiritual parent, whom we call "father" or "mother." It doesn't matter what name we use. This parent is the voice of unconditional love and forgiveness in our minds. S/He always accepts us as we are, honors others as equals, and encourages us to move through our pain and sadness. S/he never blames or judges, but empowers and forgives. We can draw comfort and strength from this voice because it is without negativity. It is always positive and uplifting.

A COURSE IN MIRACLES calls this presence that speaks to us within the Holy Spirit. There are many names for it. Perhaps you call it by a different one. That is great. All of the names for the presence of Spirit among us are beautiful.

Some might say that we who hear this voice within are simply making it up and that it has no independent existence. The latter point is probably true, but are we making it up? I suppose on some level we make everything up. Some of what we invent brings us suffering; some of it brings release from suffering.

I don't think it really matters whether we make it up or not as long as the voice we hear empowers us and helps us approach each other with greater trust. I suspect that, whenever we make something up that causes suffering, it has little to do with the voice of truth within. The voice of truth, by definition, brings only forgiveness and release from pain.

If I have an inner guide who helps me live with integrity, courage, and faith, then I would be wise to listen to him even though I may not know how he comes to be there. Let me judge him, if I must, by the results he brings into my life.

I believe it was Marx who said that "religion is the

opiate of the masses." Surely this evaluation of spirituality is similar to the one I grew up with as a child. It discounts the power of belief and imagination.

For years I listened to my parents and other atheists laud the efforts of science. In time, they maintained, science would be able to explain everything in the universe. There would be no room for superstition or beliefs in some supernatural power.

Now, of course, I realize that science is simply a set of assumptions and beliefs. Even within the world of science, there are radically different assumptions about where we have come from and where we are going. Each system of beliefs has its limitations and its strengths. Certain assumptions of mathematics and physics are necessary if you want to launch a rocket into space. A different set of assumptions is necessary if you need to deal with some tragic event in your life.

In my atheist days, I would have said: "I'd rather confront the naked truth than entertain illusions." Not surprisingly perhaps, I still feel the same way. The difference is that now I don't assume that any one set of assumptions is illusion-free. To think that religion entertains more illusions than science, is just a strange conceit.

Don't misunderstand me. I am no advocate of manipulative religious organizations that preach the dogma of sin and punishment and keep their membership in place through guilt or fear. Surely, such institutions empower me no more than the scientific materialists who make fun of them and condemn me to life without beauty, aspiration, or God.

As a child, a compassionate, hopeful word or two would have helped. Hearing something like the following would have been encouraging: "Yes, there is a power in life, a Tao, or Great Spirit, but we don't understand all of its ways. Sometimes things happen that are very difficult for us, but they don't happen because that power wants to punish us, but only so we can learn all there is to learn about life. If we listen deeply, we can sometimes hear what it is we are ready to learn. Why don't you try listening and see what happens?"

You see, I didn't need a bunch of bible stories or pat religious answers. I just needed a little bit of hope and encouragement. I needed a context large enough to contain the death of my cousin and my own eventual death. I needed to begin to explore why we are here, why we die, and what life and death really mean. I needed to take the first few hesitant steps along my own spiritual path.

I don't know why we seem to think that a child's need for spiritual exploration is less important than her need for reading, writing, math or science skills. In my opinion, there is no more important area for exploration.

The spiritual journey can be facilitated but it cannot be taught. By nature it develops curiosity and self-reliance. The ideas of other people are just the building blocks. With them, there is no limit to the types of structures children can create. When encouraged, each child will find a unique " way of being in the world" that feels safe and challenging too. We cannot wish him a greater gift than this.

TRUTH AS OUR COMPANION

As I have become more comfortable with the inner dialogue, the voice within has taken on less the character of a forgiving parent and more the character of a supportive friend. Whereas before he primarily helped me rediscover my self-love and respect after some difficult life experience, now he also encourages me to see how I attract the lessons I need for my growth. He still tells me I am not to blame, nor is anyone else. But he wants me to embrace my lessons, even if they are difficult ones. He wants me to take responsibility for what I am creating on a daily basis in my life.

This is my daily curriculum within the larger universal course I am taking. These are the specific things I need to learn, obstacles I need to overcome, or beliefs and assumptions I need to release. Whatever upsets me is grist for the mill of my learning process. It is not someone taking advantage of me. It is not God punishing me. It is me attracting the perfect lesson.

My inner friend does not take my choices away. He advises me and then lets me make the choice I want. When I make a choice that honors me, he is the first to congratulate me. When I make a choice that brings pain into my life, he is the first to remind me of the alternative I rejected. He does this not to blame me for my mistake, but to show me where correction lies.

Increasingly, I sense there are three active persons in the drama of my life. There is me, there is you, and there is the voice of truth, or whatever you might want to call it. Everything else is just part of the lesson I'm learning. Even my ego, which seems so obtuse and unmanageable, is just part of the lesson. It is there only because I keep identifying with it, and I keep doing so only out of guilt. As soon as I am willing to let go of guilt, the need for the lesson disappears, because nothing further separates me from you or from God.

All mistakes arise from the perception of separation and all lessons challenge that perception. That is why lessons are learned first in our minds. Only then does our behavior change. Behavioral programs that set up a system of rewards and punishments can produce desired short-term results, but in the long run they fail, because the changes they produce are not voluntary ones.

Change is meaningful only when I desire to change. God does not beat me when I take a direction that is contrary to my growth or reward me when I make good decisions. He simply helps me to see where my actions lead and to decide if that's where I want to go. He does not try to influence my decision. If he did, his love and faith in me would not be unconditional.

If I love you unconditionally, I must not be attached to the choice you make. I must trust you to make whatever choice you need to make. I will feel compassion if that choice hurts you or anyone else. But I will not be responsible for it.

True love for you does not mean that I become responsible for your actions. It simply means that my love for you does not depend on what you do or neglect to do. Such love is rare in this world, because it looks past all appearances into the soul of each being.

We think God wants us to feel guilty, but this is ridiculous. What would God achieve through our guilt? As long as we feel guilty, we cannot reflect Her love. The only way that we can reflect Her love is to love ourselves and others unconditionally. That is how we honor Her.

So, here we are, you, me, and our eternal friend, whose companionship we share. My guilt invites you to attack and yours invites me. My attack on you secures my guilt and your attack on me secures yours. Meanwhile, our friend looks on in astonishment. Can't we see how we spin the strands of our web of illusion?

The fact is that we don't. That's why we need our friend to walk with us. We need to be continually reminded of our innocence. We need to be continually forgiven for our attack. That is all the inner dialogue is all about. There's nothing esoteric or glamorous about it.

When I neglect the inner dialogue, I do not feel the presence of Spirit in my life. Once that happens, it doesn't take long for me to forget who I am and who you are. I get lost in the illusion of my mistaken beliefs. I forget that we are equal. I intimidate you or allow you to manipulate me. I struggle. I hurt. I separate myself from you.

So I need to remember my companion. I cannot truly get through my life without remembering this being of light and love within me.

I think that we all have different metaphors for the presence of truth in our lives. I don't think those differences are so important. What is important is that we follow our guide through all of the challenges of our lives, learning those gestures of forgiveness that release us from confusion and suffering.

Let me not question the form your guide takes if s/he leads you to joy. Let me be unconcerned if your beliefs are different from mine. If you treat me with love and respect, what more can I ask?

The form of truth varies from time to time and place to place. But its content is the same. Truth always lifts me up, but never at your expense, nor does it praise you by putting me down. Guilt is not part of its vocabulary, nor is envy or fear. What it gives to me, it gives you equally.

It is amazing that we can fight over truth. But as long as we do, we cannot live in truth, because to live in truth is to live at peace with ourselves and others.

Truth without peace is not truth, but attack. Instead of contesting each other's beliefs, let us turn our attention to the place within where peace abides. If we will enter fully there, we will find that, regardless of what is argued, truth belongs to us equally. It lives within us like a silent flame that brightens when we offer each other caring and concern. All whom we include within the circle of our love and acceptance are witnesses to our light. As such, they offer us as great a gift as we offer them.

FEAR OF DANCING

Only once in my life have I been unafraid to dance. It was in college. Henry, the guy in the room next door, was from Uganda. He stayed very much to himself, except when he was with his girlfriend. But I liked Henry. I talked to him from time to time and discovered we both liked jazz.

One night I brought a bunch of jazz albums over to his room. While we were listening to Louis Armstrong, I started to move to the music spontaneously. Henry and his girlfriend started clapping their hands, egging me on. I really got into it, letting my mind go into the music and letting the music flow out through my body. After about half an hour, I collapsed on the floor exhausted.

It was no doubt a very comical scene. Here we were the three of us, all loners, like characters out of a Beckett novel, playing music loud and whooping it up in Henry's room. Yet, for some reason, in that moment I was totally unselfconscious and relaxed. I suppose that is because I knew at some very deep level that I would not be laughed at or judged.

Henry was the only black student at my school. He was also from a different culture. I think he was also about ten years older than most of the students. All these differences kept him apart from others, probably as much by his choice as by theirs. In my own way, I felt as isolated as Henry did. Unlike me, most of the kids came from wealthy families. A lot of them were taking drugs and into popular culture. I wasn't interested in either.

My friendship with Henry was a very simple one. It was based on mutual respect. It was that respect that made it possible for me to dance in his room. It was that respect that enabled him to open up to me more than he had to anyone else at the school.

While growing up, I was very shy. I didn't reveal myself to others easily. I used to think that I was the only person in the world who was so reticent. It took me many years to realize that everybody has similar fears. Some people just do a better job of disguising them than others.

It's a lot easier to work through your fears when you know that other people have them too. I think that's the beauty of twelve step groups. They create an atmosphere in which people feel safe revealing themselves. They aren't afraid that their testimony will be judged by others or used against them. Everyone who shares is vulnerable.

Many of us think and act as if we live in a magic bubble that might pop at any moment. "If you really knew me, you wouldn't like me," we think. So we're always trying to hide something from each other. We're always trying to impress and perform. The idea of revealing our fears and our weaknesses is social suicide.

Yet intimacy is not possible unless we are willing to be vulnerable with one another. That vulnerability not only builds emotional bridges between us, but it enables us to see that others are just as afraid of being judged as we are. If I am not alone in my fears, then I do not have to feel guilty for having them and I won't have to spend all my time and energy trying to cover those fears up.

If it's okay for me to be afraid, then I can be with my fear and begin to move through it. As I do so, I can share with others so that they too will be inspired to acknowledge and move through their fears.

It is amazing how liberating it is to talk about what scares me. Now I don't have to drink my fear, or smoke my fear, or snort my fear or binge on it. I just have to acknowledge it.

Trusting others with this kind of information about yourself is not an easy proposition, especially if you have grown up doubting yourself and feeling cut off from other people. Yet the more you hold yourself back, the harder it is to share.

The first person who begins talking in a dyad or group "breaks the ice." That ice can sometimes be very thick, and the person who breaks it needs to trust that whatever s/he says will be okay. Often it is hard to go from silence into intimate sharing, and a simple comment like "boy, this was a tough week" helps to ease people into their hearts.

I remember one particularly profound group session that started with such a simple comment. And then each person who spoke shared something more intimate until everyone in the group had made a profound contribution. People really listened to each other. They let each person who spoke before them open the door to something new within. In most cases, they had no idea what they were going to say. It just evolved in their hearts out of the dialogue and they were willing to share what came up for them with the group.

When this happens, the presence of Spirit is palpable in a group. Guidance moves steadily from one mind to another, and many seemingly separate struggles during the week become clarified and surrounded in light. Without knowing it, one person's witness becomes a beacon for another. It is an amazing process. To me, the dance of life begins when we are ready to risk who we are with one another. Listening to each other deeply opens our hearts to Spirit so that we can give and receive the awareness we need.

Spirit never dances in a formal way. What it does today will be different tomorrow. Each day requires trust, because each day the dance will be new.

Dancing is hard if you need to be in control. The real dancers in life are the ones who are not afraid to trust their bodies to the music, to let their partners come and go, and to let the invisible energy of life lift their arms and feet.

DANCING WITH GOD
IN THE MIRROR OF LIFE

I must admit, I have spent most of my life trying to keep separate from you. I have tried to find a safe niche, where I could keep our interactions manageable and polite. Whenever problems have come up between us, I have moved away from you.

I keep trying to protect this "image of self" I have. I am convinced that you will reject me if I let you see behind "the pasteboard mask" I wear. I am afraid that you will see how ridiculous I am. Like my friend Don Quixote, I take my ideas and exploits seriously. I do not want you to laugh at me.

When I think you are laughing at me, I strike back at you. When you leave me alone, I campaign for your attention. I guess I am pretty confused. When you are here with me, I can't wait for you to leave. And when you leave, I miss you.

Sound familiar? Push-pull, push-pull, push-pull. This is the rhythm of life in three dimensional reality. We become co-dependent and reactionary in our interactions.

But let's not despair. We do not position ourselves in this manner just to tear each other apart. We do so to learn to see ourselves more clearly. Each interaction we have with one another offers us another glimpse into ourselves.

We begin to look at the games we are playing, not so that we can defeat each other, but so we can learn that the outcome is both certain and undesirable. Those who play the game always lose it, because the purpose of the game is to teach us to stop playing it. Games of power are addicting. Our emotions ride up and down. But no matter how high we fly, the game always lets us off at ground level. This is tough for many of us to take.

We bought into the illusion of flight. We believed in an easy ride to the top. We thought we could do it all without any struggle.

For most of us, that's not a helpful expectation. Our struggle serves a purpose. It helps to build an awareness. If we don't "struggle" against our struggle, we can actually begin to make reasonable progress in our lives.

Life throws us many curves. There's always some unidentified flying object coming our way, and it is rarely a space ship. In retrospect, all we remember is that something hit us upside the head. We just didn't see it coming. Next time, we'll be more alert.

Each one of us is involved in a great drama, in which we play all of the parts. The play seems so real, we forget it's just a play, even though we helped to build the scenery and write the script. And then we need to take a break and go out into the audience and look back in.

Gradually, we begin to get the picture. I call it "dancing in the mirror of life." That's what we all are doing. We keep forgetting the whole performance has been staged for our benefit.

As one who tends to take life fairly seriously, I do not use this metaphor flippantly. It's just that I've spent enough time in the audience to know that every so called "life and death struggle" is just the play of consciousness learning to be responsible for itself.

Every move I make is one of self-discovery, including all those moves that make me self-preoccupied and unhappy. It's all part of the process. My sadness, guilt, fear, envy, unworthiness, all of it is part of the play. And I go in and out of identifying with it. When I identify strongest, I am the most unhappy. When I learn to let go, I am filled with wonder and joy.

No, I am not who I think I am. I am not limited by the limits I place in my way unless I refuse to step beyond them. Often, to step beyond them means to step into the unknown. That is what I must do when I leave the body behind. That is what I must do when I leave behind any attachment that no longer serves me.

Let's not be ungenerous. Life after all is about attachment and detachment. Neither aspect of the process is more important than the other. They are both essential. Every cycle in our lives teaches both movements. Every breath we take teaches us to grab on and to let go. Without the polarities, the process could not exist. Yet the polarities are only reference points. Most of our lives are lived in the middle. So I am born and I die. Both the beginning and the end are a mystery. That is as is should be. Who would have energy for this journey if every movement were defined?

The mystery of birth and death move through every gesture of our lives. That is the golden thread interwoven in the tapestry. It holds it all together till it is time to undo what we have knit. And then one last breath, one little tug on the thread pulls the tapestry apart.

Every design is beautiful, yet there is not a single one that survives. For each was meant for learning only and not for all time. For, in eternity, there is no beginning or end. Only here are these reference points meaningful, for they outline the boundaries of what we know. And every moment we must cross one of those boundaries!

Without each other's help, this would not be possible. Indeed, without our mutual conspiracy, this world could not exist. We make it together. It is our tentative creation. And all of its pain and suffering are for naught if we do not remember that they are meant to bring us from darkness to light.

Yes, there is a direction. And every step into darkness is also a step toward the light. And every moment of struggle is also a movement toward surrender. Those who listen deeply do not feel betrayed by the polarities of life, but remain where they are until they pass through the tunnel.

Love does not come cheap. It comes as I master my fear. Until I do, my love for you is conditional on your behavior toward me. It is love-hate, push-pull. Only when I have had the courage to look behind the mask I wear and invite you in, do I stand with you in true relation. In the nakedness of that encounter, there are no winners or losers, for that is where the game ends. From that moment, there is the awareness that power is equal and can only be shared.

Until then I dance alone, self-conscious, for I anticipate your judgment of me. Until then, I silently judge every move you make. I attack you with the power I think you have over me, and you follow suit.

But when the power struggle ends and peace arrives, I am your partner in the dance of life. No one is better than the other. We are not here to impress others with our separate skills, but to bring our skills together into a common cause. Our progress can no longer be separately discerned, for the mis-step of one affects the other, and impedes the flow of the dance.

For partners in the dance, accommodation must be mutual. Each needs the other's help and the other's trust, and must give what s/he would receive. It's not that someone's keeping score — to be sure, such a move would interrupt the dance — but there is a flow back and forth that needs to be honored. As long as it is, the dance is effortless and smooth.

Looking back, I see that my efforts to stay separate from you were just an exercise in resistance. I thought the journey was about meeting your ego needs or mine. Now that I know it isn't about either, I am beginning to find fewer excuses for not joining the dance.

No, nobody is holding a gun to my head. It isn't like that. I just don't see the purpose of staying back. If my lesson is about equality, I can learn it only by joining in. Sure my feet will get stepped on and I'll mistakenly tread on someone else's toes, but that's the only way to learn the dance.

The more trust I bring to my partner, the easier it is. Knowing the right moves is only the beginning of it. It just helps me trust myself more so I can bring that trust to you.

I can't dance with God until I have learned to trust myself and my partner. Yet trust is not a black and white proposition. It is an inner softening and letting go, a little on one side and then on the other. Now there is a bit of rhythm, a bit of flow. Now we enter into that rhythm more confidently, extending it, playfully.

In time, we forget that we are the ones dancing. Indeed, it seems the dance is dancing us. And then we know that God has joined the dance. And then we know that God is the dance, and that only by dancing it have we found Him.

❁

Part Seven

Every Flower Needs Water

THE PROCESS OF ATTUNEMENT

I once took a timberframing workshop out in the Berkshires. Before beginning our work for the day, we all gathered in a circle and held hands with eyes closed. These few moments of silence helped us to relax, come into the present moment, and become aware of one another.

It was a simple, but invaluable ritual. It helped us begin our day with a positive regard for one another and appreciation for the work at hand. It helped the building process go more smoothly and enabled us to avoid accidents.

When I do workshops and classes, I often begin with this simple ritual. When many people come into a room, they are mentally in different places. The attunement helps us come together in recognition of why we are here as individuals and as a group.

A similar type of attunement can be experienced in individual meditation by allowing all of the contents of consciousness to reveal themselves without judgment. When thoughts are not resisted, they settle down, revealing a deep silence. This is the space in which our guidance spontaneously arises.

I have said many times that our guidance is present if we are willing to listen to it. But we forget that listening is a skill. We do not know how to listen deeply anymore, not to ourselves or to each other. For, to listen deeply, means to listen without judgment.

If I know what I am listening for, then I am not listening. I am projecting my thoughts. If I am troubled about something, my thoughts will be troubled, and the answer I hear will be part of the problem. I will not experience an inner calm or sense of release.

Listening means putting the problem out there and detaching from it. I am not the problem. I am the person experiencing the problem. The answer to the problem comes from me. It does not come from the problem or from the consciousness identified with the problem. It comes from a consciousness that is problem free. Just for a moment, then, let me let go of the problem. I can always have it back if I want it.

Let me just be with the problem and know that I am not the problem. I don't have to minimize it or exaggerate it. I just need to be with it and see it apart from me. Let me not try to solve the problem. Let me be willing to abide with the problem without needing to do something about it.

Now I begin to accept myself at a deeper level. Now I begin to listen to the "me" who is whole and intact. Now, I begin to see things differently. Perhaps the problem just disappears. Or perhaps I discover an unexpected way to resolve it. The solution comes "out of the blue." There is no deliberation or evaluation. Something suggests itself and it feels right.

Hearing our guidance is an inner attunement. It is a bringing of our minds into heart-level awareness. There is a deep sense of relaxation, a deep sense of peace.

Most of our lives are lived at the edge of consciousness, where we are striving for certain results. Inner attunement brings us back to the center of consciousness, where there is no striving. When we come from this center, we are able to address the outward challenges of our lives with purpose and with grace.

Central to the attunement process is the recognition that I am okay right now just as I am. I don't have to change anything about my life. Everything is okay. Even the things I think I want to change are okay as they are. Even my wanting to change those things is okay. I accept my lack of acceptance.

There is a beautiful quote written by one of Ragneesh's disciples. My friend Rupa has it in her meditation room. It says:

> A Synnasin does not escape, and if
> he does, he does not beat himself for that,
> and if he beats himself, he does not feel
> guilty about that, and if he does, he
> accepts that he does so, and if he can't
> accept that, he accepts that he doesn't ac-
> cept it.

It doesn't matter how long it takes us to catch hold of the thread of self-acceptance, so long as we embrace it somewhere. With all of the judgment tapes we are constantly running in our minds, catching hold of the single thought that brings us peace is not easy. But it is essential to our spiritual practice. We can't love others without feeling loving and accepting of ourselves.

Any person who chooses to walk the spiritual path is involved in an ongoing process of self-forgiveness. It is the only thing that calms the mind and awakens an inner joy and well being.

There is nothing particularly complicated about this process. It is just hard to do, because it reverses the whole train of negative thoughts steaming through the mind at ninety miles an hour. It says: "Okay slow down and let me look at one car at a time." And it sees that every car is a negative thought, followed by another, and another, and another. And then it says: "these thoughts can't be doing me any good. Let me start with one positive thought, one thought that honors me right here and now." And, that's how the train turns around. The engine gets put on the other side and the train starts moving in a positive direction.

We all do this from time to time when we rebound from depression, but we may not be aware that we are the ones who turn the train around. Yet, at a certain point in our journey, we realize that we are the engineer, the conductor, and the passenger to boot. If the train goes out of control, it is because we have fallen asleep on the job.

We have heard the phrase "love and accept yourself" so often, it begins to sound trite. But the process of learning to do this is anything but trite. It is hard work. It involves constant self-witnessing. In A COURSE IN MIRACLES, it says "be vigilant for God and His Kingdom." The self-witnessing and forgiveness process is an essential aspect of that vigilance.

❁

BRINGING PRACTICE INTO THE PRESENT

It is not enough to know intellectually that we are innocent in our heart of hearts. We must begin to experience that innocence. One way to do this is to witness negative thoughts. The witnessing process helps us uncover the space behind our negativity, which is free of judgment.

Our spirituality does not have to involve getting rid of negative thoughts. That is too much to expect. But it does have to involve becoming aware of such thoughts.

Our spirituality does not have to involve getting rid of all the highs and lows we experience. But it does have to involve becoming aware of them.

In our awareness, we ground our ascent and cushion our fall. We stay centered in the midst of change.

To be sure, we are not aware in every moment. We forget to witness. We find ourselves attaching to a desire, a thought, an image of another or of ourselves, or we find ourselves crashing against a wall when that idea or image proves illusory.

And then we remember that we are here to listen and to learn, and our attention returns to the present moment. As long as we keep bringing our attention back, we remain on the path.

In meditation, we go through the same process in microcosm. Our attention wanders and we bring it back. It wanders again, and again we bring it back. Thoughts begin to slow down. The space between them widens. Now we see each thought come, register in the mind like a stone cast in a pool of water, and we see its effects, like ripples in the pool.

Instead of a freight train moving ninety miles an

hour, our thoughts are a slow dance, like yoga asanas or Tai Chi movements. And we are the dancer and the one watching the dance.

All of life is a meditation when we slow up the train of our thoughts and begin to remember our purpose here. Special times and places for meditation, while helpful, are not necessary.

A Meditative life is simply one lived in awareness of one's own states of consciousness. Awareness helps us take responsibility for our thoughts and their translation into three dimensions.

Not long ago, I took my children out for breakfast. Next to the breakfast place was a park with animals. I wanted the kids to see the animals, but I didn't want to pay the high admission price. Since the breakfast place was adjacent to the park, it was easy to walk in. We did.

We had a really nice time in the park and, as we were walking back, I thought that I really wanted to pay as a way of saying thank you. Just then, one of the owners came out and confronted me for not paying. I felt really embarrassed. She correctly pointed out that I was not setting a very good example for the children.

To me this was a perfect example of life saying to me "there is never a time when you are off-duty. Every decision you make is a blessing to yourself and others or an attempt to escape responsibility."

I'm not especially proud of this situation, but it was a strong lesson for me. More and more, my lessons come to me immediately after I make a mistake. I don't have to wait two or three years for the chickens to come home to roost. They often return within hours.

If I want to be open to my lessons, I can't

disregard the ones that are difficult for me or refuse to share the ones that do not show me in a positive light. I make mistakes just as you do. Why hide my mistakes?

Recently, in a workshop I was giving for students of A COURSE IN MIRACLES, one of the participants interrupted the discussion: "I thought you were going to teach us some stuff, Paul," she said, obviously exasperated with what we were discussing.

"I don't really have anything to teach you that you don't already know," I replied. I'm here to share about my life and what I'm learning and to encourage you to do the same. I'm not here as someone who has answers you don't have. We all have the same amount of knowledge here. It's just a question of whether we're willing to trust it and apply it to our lives. If I share my lessons with you, it empowers you to learn your own."

Sharing helps me overcome the sense of separation I often feel. It helps me realize that I am not alone with my lessons. Many of my friends feel just as vulnerable as I do. We all stumble in different places, or in the same places at different times. Our witness to Spirit in our lives is very important.

Sharing with each other from the heart is as important a spiritual practice as self-witnessing. The early Christians knew this. That is what the ritual of confession was originally about. People came together as equals to talk about their mistakes and how they were learning from them. They did not come to judge, but to draw inspiration from each other's lives.

Too often we avoid intimate group experiences because we are afraid that others will judge us. Usually, it is the other way around. These groups help us confront our judgments about other people. And as we do that, we see that we are making the same judgment about ourselves.

We need to learn again what it means to be vulnerable with one another. I don't have to be perfect in your eyes to be worthy of your love, and you don't have to be perfect in mine. We all make mistakes. We all feel bad about certain thoughts or behaviors. And we all suffer silently with our guilt when we need to call out to each other for love and support.

Self acceptance is one half of our practice. Acceptance of each other is the other half. When Jesus said that one of the two greatest commandments is "love your neighbor as yourself," he underscored the importance of practicing our equality.

The experience of equality does not come naturally to the ego. It must be cultivated in our interactions. Surely that is why we are here together.

Loving myself helps me approach you as an equal. But I am not perfect in my love for myself, so I will not be perfect in loving you. Every time I misperceive you, you will either react to my attack, or remind me of your innocence by showing me my own. That is your choice, and mine as well.

This is an amazing practice. Every time I feel attacked I am offered the opportunity to love. Jesus did not say "love your friends." He said "love your enemies." If that isn't a spiritual practice, I don't know what is.

I cannot love my enemy unless I see myself in him. His weaknesses, his fears, his sorrows are not so different from my own. I must reach deeply into my love for myself to love him. I must be willing to forgive myself for everything I think he has done to me.

Every success I have strengthens my practice. Every failure offers me another chance to find the light of forgiveness. I will never completely learn this lesson, for there will never be a time when forgiveness is not necessary.

Time and forgiveness go hand in hand. Only She who knows Herself perfect without exception no longer needs to forgive Herself. She is here in time, yet beyond it. To Her we turn when we need comfort and encouragement, for She never wavers in her love for us.

✪

REMEMBERING TO WATER THE PLANTS

Sometimes I forget to water my plants. The leaves begin to turn yellow and they look forlorn. For a moment I wonder why. Then I remember that I have neglected them.

When my plants are healthy, my life is healthy. I have the energy to notice when they need my attention. I am relaxed and able to respond.

It is a simple thing, perhaps. Yet I know of no more important barometer of the state of my life. When I forget to tend to my plants, you can be sure I have forgotten to tend to myself.

So many of us get lost in our daily responsibilities. We have so much to do, we never take time for ourselves. The harder we work, the harder we have to work. It is a vicious cycle.

We all need to step back for a few moments. We need to slow down and ask "where am I going?" If we are honest, we'll see that we aren't going anywhere in particular. We think we are moving ahead in some linear sequence toward some goal, but in truth we are just turning in place.

We keep telling ourselves "when I get there, I'll relax. Then I'll have time to be at peace and enjoy myself." It is like those two Beckett characters who are waiting for Godot. Everything in their lives is arranged around the expectation of Godot's arrival, yet Godot never shows up. In the same way, all our activities are arranged around the idea of some future happiness which never arrives.

No matter how hard we try — and we try very, very hard — happiness just can't be found in the future. Happiness is now or it is not now, but it is never in the future. Perhaps it seems foolish to ask the question:

"Am I happy now?" Yet what better question can I ask?

If I am not happy, then no amount of striving will make me happy. I can get very busy searching for happiness, so busy in fact that I completely cut myself off from the little opportunities for joy that are available to me.

I try to be responsible for so many things, so many people, but I forget to be responsible for my present happiness. If I am not responsible for my present happiness, then all the responsibilities I take on will just lead me away from myself.

If life seems difficult, stressful, or hollow, it is because I have moved away from my joy. I have put it on hold.

Joy is a funny thing, when you put it on hold, it just disappears. It doesn't hang around waiting for you to use it when you get time. If you don't use it, you lose it.

Happiness can only be tasted in the moment. It comes and goes. If you don't enjoy it when it comes, you are a masochist. Who knows when it will come again?

I am not saying it won't come again. Of course it will! But every time you reject it, you position further yourself away from its path. The longer you postpone joining, the more separation seems to deepen, until you feel totally cut off, totally imprisoned.

Of course, you have the same access to joy then that you always had. It just feels to you like you don't. Psychologically, it becomes harder to embrace life.

Postponing joy programs the mind for separation and failure. When I recognize that, it doesn't seem so outrageous to ask the question "Am I happy now?" And if the answer is no, then I have a simple but direct challenge: "Right now, let me be responsible for my own happiness."

Let me put my struggle aside for a few moments. Let me take a walk, or do some deep breathing, or think of something inspirational. If there is something I really want to do, let me give myself permission to do it.

You may ask this question and respond to it only once during the day, but it will be a moment you remember. For that moment, you stopped putting joy on hold. You stopped cramming your mind with expectations and tasks to perform. For that moment, you relaxed and let your energy unfold.

You know, I believe each one of us is like a plant. Our needs are very simple. We need a little attention, a little water when we are thirsty. Why is it so hard for us to give ourselves that attention? Why do we bury our heads in the sand with mountains of cares and concerns and neglect the flower within us, whose needs are so simple?

There is a book by a Zen Master called "A Flower Does not Talk." I don't think that is completely true. Nevertheless, if a flower does talk, it speaks to us so softly we can barely hear it. The flower of Spirit is that way. It does not yell and scream and demand our attention. It just waits quietly for us to attend to it. Sometimes its leaves wither and we wonder why it is not putting forth new shoots, and then we remember we have not given it water in over a week. Is it any wonder that we feel tired and stressed out?

The flower of Spirit thrives on joy. If there is not joy in our lives right now, the flower needs to be tended. Let us put other responsibilities aside and give the flower what it needs. For, without joy, those responsibilities cannot be fulfilled.

Without my present happiness, my future goals mean very little. Joy is the water of life. It feeds me now. It feeds you. And it feeds all beings.

A world without joy is a barren world, a desert where nothing grows. How can we settle for such a world? How can we live our lives in its shadow? No, we were meant to live a different life. We were meant to build a different world, a world where our gifts can be freely given and received, a world where the soil is fertile and worked with love.

Every person has an inner garden and his first responsibility is to tend to it. If he does, he can feed himself, and have enough to share with those who are still hungry. To tend that garden does not require a lot of material wealth, but it does require faith in one's self and in the gift one has to give.

Without that faith, the seeds of life will be sown too close to the surface, where they will bake in the sun. With it, those seeds will be more deeply sown, where they will find the water they need to nurture them. Then, they will take root and gather the strength to poke their fragile bodies through the dark earth into the light of day. That is the creative process.

We all belong to it. Yet many of us walk away from it, alienating ourselves from the source of our happiness. Let's not forget that we can come back to it when we are ready. We just need to remember that "right now, right here, in spite of all of the burdens I carry, I have but one responsibility, and that is to do what I love, to move toward my joy."

COMMUNICATION AND PURPOSE
IN RELATIONSHIPS

Often, when something feels wrong in our lives, we have difficulty acknowledging it and communicating our feelings to the appropriate people. We are afraid that people will judge our feelings or react to them with their own.

I remember one relationship I had in which my partner was not very responsive in bed. She didn't resist sex, but rarely initiated it, and didn't seem to be completely enjoying it, even though she did climax regularly. During one particular stretch of time, she made minimal effort to arouse me and, as a result, I had difficulty getting and maintaining an erection.

I felt really upset and finally told her so. I said that having sex with her felt like rape, because she didn't seem to be emotionally involved in it. I said that I wasn't able to perform sexually unless I felt that the other person really wanted me. To honor myself, I felt I would have to stop having sex with her until I was convinced that she wanted to make love with me.

All this wasn't easy for me to say. My goal was certainly not to stop having sex with her, nor was I interested in finding another sexual partner. I wanted her, but only if she also wanted me. Mutuality was the key.

Fortunately, my willingness to communicate how I felt really helped our relationship. My partner became much more present in our lovemaking, and it became more enjoyable for both of us. Yet, even if the result had been different, the communication was essential for me. I knew what I needed and I had to honor that. Accepting a situation that was not empowering to me would have been disastrous for me, and ultimately for my partner too.

Rarely, in any relationship is dissatisfaction felt on just one side. One person may be more in touch with discomfort than the other, but exploration will reveal that both people have expectations of the other that are not being met.

Whatever I expect of the other person, I expect of myself. If I am willing to give what I desire in return, then my expectation is fair. Whether or not the other person can meet that expectation is another story.

It is unfair to demand that anyone meet our expectations. Each person has the right to say yes or no to us. That right cannot be challenged.

We, in turn, have the right to say what is important to us. If the other person is unable or unwilling to respond, we have the right to seek others who can meet our needs. Yet, we should realize that our needs cannot be met until we are willing to give to others what we would receive from them.

My partner's expectation was that I be more helpful around the house. She felt that my lack of help was a message that I did not value her. Since I did value her, I was willing to find a way to show it that she appreciated.

It is very difficult to have a relationship unless both people feel that their needs are heard and responded to. To achieve this goal, communication is essential, especially when things get difficult. The harder it is to communicate, the more important it is to do so.

All relationships get in a groove. Partners begin to take each other for granted. They stop talking about their feelings and concerns. The relationship becomes stale. It needs new blood. Although disconcerting at first, the expression of strong emotion from one or both partners can often be a wake up call for them. Inevitably, emotions such as anger are a call for love. They say to the other person: "don't take me for granted. Listen to me. See me as I am."

Fairness and negotiation skills are essential for any relationship to prosper. Yet other aspects are also important. Partners should have a vision of themselves together which energizes both of them. They should also be comfortable with and supportive of each other's life purpose.

A relationship between people who do not appreciate each other's unique needs and talents cannot flourish. If it remains intact as a structure, it becomes a mutual prison, preventing each person from developing emotionally, intellectually, and spiritually. Such a price is too high to pay for both people.

Relationships are learning devices. They exist in our lives to build consciousness. Yet, they are also vehicles for the expression of our light and love. The best relationships challenge us and nurture us at the same time. They strengthen and support us emotionally so that we can begin to overcome our limited thinking and our lingering fears.

When a relationship loses its balance between challenge and nurturing, it becomes either too threatening or too restrictive. Communication is essential then so that the balance can be regained.

A COURSE IN MIRACLES talks about special relationships. In a special relationship, the partners are co-dependent. Any relationship that binds is special. Any relationship that releases is holy. In a special relationship I ask you to meet my needs. In a holy relationship, I am content to meet my needs and happy to meet yours if I can do so with energy and purpose. But, if meeting your needs means betraying my own, then I am not willing to do it. If I do, I am bound to resent it, and I am likely to expect you to make a similar sacrifice.

Part of our learning in this world involves transforming our special relationships into holy relationships. I do not do this by denying my needs or sacrificing anything that is important to me. I do this by honoring myself at all times, and honoring you, even when your needs are different from mine. I remain faithful to myself, and I bid you do the same. I celebrate when we come together in common purpose, and I let go when our purposes seem to divide.

I know that each of us must follow our own path. Sometimes, it is helpful to travel together. Sometimes, it is helpful to move on by ourselves. There is no need to judge either choice, for each has its appropriate time and place in our lives.

Somewhere there is a saying "hold on tightly; let go lightly." There is nothing more wonderful than an embrace that is entirely open and mutual. There is nothing more touching than saying goodbye with love in our hearts.

SUDDEN PARTINGS

Recently, one of my brother's close friends died suddenly. He got pneumonia and had complications. He was only thirty-six.

Around the same time, a relative of my wife also died. He was in his eighties and had lived a full live. He was a person who loved the outdoors and was always very active. He had come to Arizona to be with his close friends. I guess he needed to say goodbye. His condition forced him to have a machine that helped him to breathe. One morning, after his visitors left, he pulled the plug on his machine.

This morning I was talking with my son about both situations. "You know, the body doesn't last forever," I told him. "When people get old and their bodies don't work so well and they have a lot of pain, they may not want to live any longer. That's what happened to Bert. He knew he wouldn't enjoy life any more. He would just be a burden to himself and others. It was time for him to move on and he accepted it."

"What's it like to die?" my son asked me.

"I don't know," I said, "but some people who have come very close to dying say that it's like going through a dark tunnel. You can see light at the other end. When you come to the end of the tunnel, you see all the people you loved who have died before you, and you feel their love. And you feel the love of God and the power of the light which is all around you."

"If that's what it's like," my son said, "then I really wouldn't mind dying."

"I wouldn't either," I said. "I just hope that when I die I'm not afraid. I hope I can leave my body a few times before I die so I know what it's like. And then when it's time for me to die, I can let go and experience the whole thing."

"That would be neat," he said.

"Yeah," I said. "I want to be awake when I die. I want to die consciously and without fear."

Every time to time, sudden partings like that of my brother's friend make me aware of my own mortality. Usually, when the thought of my own death comes up, I feel that I'm not ready to die and just dismiss it. "I can't die now;" I say to myself, "I have too much to do."

Of course, I realize that this is probably a weak argument, but it helps me avoid thinking about death. Thinking about death invariably invokes some degree of fear in me. I think of my life just ending without whim or purpose. Or I see myself getting older and approaching death as some sort of unwelcome fiat I must confront.

I would like to be ready for death when it is time to die, but my fear is that I won't, that I'll want to hold on. My fear is that I'll be a coward, that I'll betray my own values and beliefs.

But every once and a while, a different image of death comes up. In this image, I have completed all that I wanted to do in my life and there's really no reason to continue here. Those whose companionship I need for my growth have already left their bodies behind. I have a sense of completion, and an expectation of rebirth. I am relaxed and at peace.

To be in such a place, even for a moment or two, is a great blessing. It helps me overcome my fears of annihilation. It is an extraordinary thought: "Yes, perhaps I will not die until I am ready to."

"That I could live with," I say to myself, much as my son said to me when he heard my description of dying. I guess I need to hold a positive image of death for myself as well as for him.

The thought that I will be ready for death, just as I have been ready for the things that have happened in my life, is a liberating one. It means that I come to death willingly. And if this is true, then death too is part of the journey I have chosen to take. It is not the end of the journey, but a waystation, where I can rest and get ready for the next stage.

A life without purpose is not acceptable to me. Even at the moment of death, it is not acceptable. I choose to live my life with purpose because I could not live it otherwise. In that sense, I must choose to die with purpose as well.

My life and death are my signature here. They are like the words in my books. They show the way I chose to take, what I thought and how I felt. They show the judgments I made and the ones I learned to overcome. They show the moments when I made mistakes, and the moments when I learned to forgive myself.

I have recorded the song of my life so that you could listen to it as many times as you find it helpful. I have placed it before you, not as a model for you to follow, but as a reminder of how one brother lived. He was no more talented than you, nor was he possessed of any more courage. What he had, you have as well. I do not have any special knowledge. What I have, I share. The very fact that you can receive it shows that you share it too.

When my student and friend Elaine died, I felt cheated. I wanted more of her. I felt that she could heal herself. I refused to believe that she was a victim of her illness. But she died in six months, like clockwork, just like the Doctors said she would. She went

through the medical rite of passage: diagnosis —
cancer of the pancreas; treatment — chemotherapy
and radiation; prognosis — six months to a year to
live.

Elaine, I know that you did not want to die.
Death came to you and you reluctantly embraced it.
We were robbed of your presence here. Yet at times
I feel you are still here with us. Sometimes I think of
you, and I am not dwelling on your death anymore,
and I realize that you are alive in my thoughts. Even
now, we can join, for a moment. And I am thankful
for that moment, whatever it means.

When someone leaves the body, someone somewhere feels grateful for his life. There is no person
whose life lacks some small gesture of love. Life
without love is not possible, for love is the law of life.
No one breaks that law all of the time. Even if his life
is filled with transgression, there are still moments of
beauty and grace. Someone has experienced them
and someone gives thanks for those moments.

In our black and white judgments of ourselves
and others, we do not remember the love we have
given and received. Yet it is there, more deeply than
the sadness and the pain. Truth lies in the moments
when we have met without fear. It shines forth from
those moments like a lighthouse beacon, guiding us
through the fog and foul weather of our lives.

It is daybreak now on the storm-shaken beach.
A thin salmon colored light lingers on the sand and
opens with it as the tide retreats. At low tide, piles of
stones emerge that were not there before. The beach
is littered with driftwood, seaweed and old bottles.
The presence of the storm lingers, but there is a
gentleness here and a glow not seen before.

Just such a glow was present in my father's house

when my brother and I came to visit him after his second wife died. I felt her presence there as strongly as I ever had before. And there was such a sweetness in it. I had never witnessed it in full bloom when she was alive. But there, sitting in my Dad's living room, the bloom was on.

When I think of anyone with love, warmth comes into my heart. That warmth is not just my loving thought, but its reflection in the mirror of life. Somewhere, someone has received it and returned it to me softened by their touch, sweetened by their gratitude. The more I hold that thought in my heart, the more it is responded to until the entire world is enfolded in its embrace.

The love of all loving beings is present in every loving thought. And the thinking of that thought is the moment when without fear I can cross the bridge between life and death. That is the moment I promised my son, the moment of At-one-ment. May he see it in my eyes and feel it in his heart when I leave this world behind.

Part Eight

Light Without Shadows

RELEASING THE DARKNESS

It is important to understand that inner child work begins, not ends, with our ability to remember and acknowledge what happened to us as children. Yes, we must feel the pain that we have repressed for so long. We must retrace the labyrinthine journey of our unmet needs and their resulting compensatory behaviors back to their source. We must reach bottom. We must allow ourselves to become vulnerable again. As children, we must learn to say yes to ourselves and to each other. It is a healing act, an act of great importance.

Authentic inner child work is not a process of wallowing in our pain or using it to justify our unhappiness. It is not an excuse for staying wounded. The inner child can heal only to the extent that we bless ourselves at the most primary existential level and begin to take responsibility for our lives.

The child is not reclaimed if we keep him separate from us. We must integrate him into the very fabric of our being. His needs and our needs are no longer different. Our aspirations and his are no longer 180 degrees apart. It is no longer acceptable for us to ignore the child's feelings, nor is it acceptable for the child to sabotage our need to actualize our full potential. Both our feelings and our aspirations are essential aspects of our personhood. When we heal the inner child, we bring together the emotional and spiritual sides of our lives.

To be sure, there was a time for many of us when we cut off our emotions. Then, there was a huge gap between what we professed to believe and how we acted in our lives. The psyche was split. Yet our emotions refused to disappear. No matter how hard we worked to hide them, they continued to assert themselves at the most inconvenient times.

That is why we had to undertake this journey of acceptance, this journey that for many of us has gone into the darkest places of our beings. In the midst of pain and self blame, we could not pretend any longer that we were happy and well adjusted. There was a schism between our public and private selves, between conscious and unconscious.

Our journey was begun in search of integration. We could not keep running from our fears. We had to learn to face them.

So we went into the scary places, coming face to face with our negative images of self. We had to look at ourselves through the eyes of our enemies, not to punish ourselves, but to find a deeper sense of self-acceptance. We had to say, "yes, you are right, I have behaved like a fool, but I am not a fool. I am someone who hurts, someone who takes his self-hatred and tries to make you responsible for it. I see that now."

We do not enter the dark places of our psyches to blame ourselves or others, but to forgive ourselves for our mistakes and to take responsibility for not repeating them. Forgiveness without responsibility is impossible. Genuine self forgiveness leads to responsibility because it releases us from the guilt we are carrying and makes positive action possible.

In my view, too much inner child work stalls in blame and pain and does not come forward toward forgiveness and responsibility. It carries the darkness forward and uses it as an excuse for why we cannot grow and open our hearts to each other. In that sense, it can be as regressive as was Freudian analysis in its day.

When we journey into the past, we do so because our attachment to it interferes with our ability to accept ourselves in the present. Our goal is to return to the present better able to accept ourselves as we are. That means integrating our feelings back into our life. It means recognizing our vulnerability and overcoming shame so that we can acknowledge and learn from our mistakes.

We go into the past to understand and release "the hooks," not to attach to them more rigidly. We go into the past to uncover the judgments others made about us, not to punish them or to justify our negative reactions, but to understand that those judgments are unfounded. We enter the past to release guilt and shame, so that we can recover our innocence, our trust, our ability to embrace life. It is not an easy journey, but its goal is positive. If we forget the goal, we can get lost in the tunnels of judgment and blame. Darkness is addicting. Let's not forget that.

Darkness says: "It's my fault," or it says "It's not my fault; it's his fault." Darkness always makes someone wrong, because darkness is the voice of shame and blame. It is the belief that someone (you or me) is sinful and must be punished.

If I enter the darkness thinking that I am to blame and leave it thinking you are to blame, then I have taken the darkness with me. If I enter thinking you are to blame and leave thinking I am to blame, I have clothed myself in the same false belief. As long as I believe that anyone is to blame, I have not forgiven myself. And until I forgive myself, I cannot begin to take responsibility for my life.

Light is acceptance. When I see light in myself, I accept myself as I am. When I see light in you, I accept you as you are. That does not mean that either one of us is perfect. It does not mean that either one of us is free of mistakes. Quite the contrary. Both of us have carried the darkness of shame and blame with us all our lives. We have used those beliefs to attack and defend, to justify and condone.

We entered the darkness to find the root of our pain. We entered to acknowledge the part of us we have denied so long. We came to the child, not as a judgmental parent, but as a loving one. It was not easy, but it was the only approach that enabled us to let go of our suffering and pain. Only love releases. Only love brings the darkness into the light.

Loving myself means loving the part of me that is weak and afraid, the part of me that is angry and hurt, the part of me that withdraws or attacks others. Why do I have to love that part of myself? Because it exists. For no other reason. If I am in fear, I need to love the one in fear.

That's what it means to embrace my darkness and bring it to the light. That is what it means to reclaim the inner child. This is a journey through fear to love.

Yes, moving into fear is a step beyond the denial of it. But it is not the end of the process. It is where the process begins.

The process of recovery does not end until there is no one left to blame, including myself. It does not end until I see the light in myself and others.

If I have come face to face with my own fear, my own darkness, my own false beliefs, then I can look at yours without feeling threatened. I can see the hurt, the anger, the fear, the blame and the shame without judging them. I know you have to go through all this darkness to emerge in the light. I do not condemn you for it. I offer you gentle encouragement. I offer you the love you so desperately need, the love you cannot see in your judgment of self and others. I show you only the light, because I know the darkness you are carrying around is not real, except in your own eyes.

To ask you to love before you are ready would be unfair. But I can love you, without asking anything in return, because I am ready to love, and because I know that love always answers itself. I do not address the darkness in you, but the light that I know is there. By so doing, I strengthen it.

I am not afraid of the screaming child, for I have taken him in my arms and rocked him and spoken to him softly the words of love he needed to hear. I looked past his anger and his hurt. I looked past his need to blame and to shame, for there was something deeper there. Whatever darkness he offered me, I declined to accept. "I have only love to offer you, little one," I said, "for love is what you want and what you have been afraid to give. In giving it to you, I give it to myself, for you are the child I never was, and I am the father you never had."

No, I am not afraid of the screaming child in myself or in you. I know that all he asks for is love. And that is the only gift I can offer him.

LIVING IN THE CONSCIOUSNESS OF GOD'S LOVE

In the title poem of my Book AVAILABLE LIGHT, I wrote:

We are in the cocoon . . .
living without wings
in the consciousness
that gives birth to wings.

Often, I have this powerful sense that we are all okay just as we are, we just don't know it. Each one of us is doing exactly what he or she needs to do to awaken. We couldn't do a better job, even if we wanted to!

You see, it's not a question of doing something different with our lives. It is a question of doing what we are doing with energy and attention.

My life can be going just terribly, but if out of my depths I can bring energy and attention to my situation, I can free it from unnecessary struggle or inertia. Exercising my mind and finding options where choices appear to be black and white or non-existent is as important as exercising my physical body.

Like a caterpillar in a cocoon, we are involved in a process of growth which is truly awesome. We all emerge from the process with abilities we did not have before, except as potentials. Developing these new abilities is painful to us only as long as we resist the process that naturally occurs in our lives.

I don't know about you, but I am perpetually resisting my growth process. I think that I would be happier if I moved to a different place, or if I was in a different relationship, or if I were free to do something I'm afraid to do. This is a kind of game I play with myself. It keeps my life at arm's length, where I don't have to experience the intensity of its warp and woof. Because there is always the possibility of change, I don't have to fully be here.

Yet at the same time that I desire change, I am invested in keeping things as they are. Otherwise, I would decide to take the risk and make certain changes in my life. So not only do I not have to be here fully, I don't have to go anywhere else either. I'm in limbo, not here, not there. I could be doing a backfloat or swimming the crawl, but instead I'm treading water. I expend a great deal of energy going nowhere.

When I recognize this game I'm playing, I can bring my energy back into my life. I can be here more fully, or go somewhere where want to be. I can commit myself to my life. Whenever I do that, I get immediate results. I stop treading water, accept my life, and take responsibility for my growth.

Until I make this gesture, it is very difficult to speak of my relationship with God. How can God help me if I am not committed to my life? The dialogue with God begins with that commitment.

It has been my experience that God's love flows

through the channel of my love for myself. If I don't love myself, I can't feel God's love. That doesn't mean it isn't there, but it might as well not be, because I don't feel it.

For me, this is a moment to moment proposition. In the moments in which I forget to love myself, God is distant and silent. In the moments in which I remember to love myself, God is quickly at my side.

As long as I am loving myself or you, love lives in me and I abide in it. At that moment I have no fear of death or abandonment of any kind. I understand that death can take the body, but not the soul. It can take the seat of fear, but not the seat of love.

If I want to be with God, I must do so in my own consciousness. There, I prepare the altar of Spirit and meet God as his son. There I meet my brother and sister as equals. It does not happen outside. It happens in my own mind and heart.

Of course, what flowers inside also flowers without. I cannot help but reflect to you and everyone else the love in my heart. In the same way, I cannot help but reflect to you my fear. My mind is a vehicle for fear or love. I always reflect to you what I feel about myself.

When I am in fear, I am unable to be aware of God as a positive, loving presence in my life. In fact, I am actually afraid of God, without knowing it. I think I am afraid of you, or of the devil, or of some evil spirit, but really I am afraid of God. I believe that God has the power to punish me, to separate me from the source of love. But these are all things which I alone have the power to do. I have projected my capacity for separation onto God. My fear of Him is just the externalization of my fear of myself.

You are not the only target for my projections. God is an even bigger target than you!

I cannot meet God within without taking on the struggle with my own fear. I cannot feel the love that God has for me without awakening my love for myself.

Each of us must prepare an inner temple for the living God, not the God of bibles, scriptures and times past, but the God who lives right now. This temple cannot be built until fear has been faced and love welcomed. Its foundation is love, love of myself, love of you, and love of my life exactly as it is. Because it is built with the hands of love, only love can enter there. And where only love is, there God abides too.

As I live my daily life, I forget to love myself, and I lose consciousness of God's love for me. And then, after a few moments, or hours, or days of depression, I remember to love myself or to love you and I can feel God's presence in my heart again. It is an amazing thing. It is an awesome teaching!

HEALING THE WOUNDED CHILD

God's grace is apparent when we trust in His most simple lessons. After years of learning all those hard lessons life brought to me, I finally realized that the answer to all of them was self-forgiveness. I didn't have to change this attitude or that one. The need to change something about myself kept me bound to the past. I didn't need to "make myself better." I just had to forgive myself for not meeting my own expectations.

Carrying the past with us is a heavy burden. The more we carry it, the more that burden grows until we can barely move our bodies under its enormous weight. We become present casualties of past wounds. We do not realize it, but we hold our healing process at bay.

In some strange way, our wounds start to define us. They become our ego's cry for recognition and our primary reason for bonding with others. Like a group of veterans reminiscing about old war battles, we validate each other not for our innocence, but for the suffering of the past. It is easy to prolong this infant stage of the healing process.

Clearly our spiritual journey is built on the understanding that we are loved and accepted. However, as much as the wounded child needs to soak up all the love that is available to him, he must realize that the source of love is within, not without.

Support groups, at their best, demonstrate the reality of unconditional acceptance and love; they empower us to trust ourselves and actualize our life purpose. Yet, at their worst, they offer a forum for the sharing of war stories, replaying the tapes of violation over and over again, and justifying our inability to find joy in our lives here and now. At their worst, they enslave us to the past and arrest our healing process. This is a price for love and support we must not be willing to pay.

Recently, I watched a program by John Bradshaw on television. I love Bradshaw's work and feel that it is among the most important work being done in therapy and healing. Yet, I could not help but feel that there was an important piece missing. As I watched the faces of the program participants getting in touch with the pain of childhood, and mourning for the love they never received as children, it occurred to me that they were in mourning for their adulthood too. Being an adult is just as difficult as being a child in this society, especially if you have children. The economic and environmental stresses on adults who parent in our society are just as overwhelming and wounding as the ones they faced as children.

In a sense many of us are twice wounded. We must mourn not only for the childhood we never had as children, but also for the adulthood we never had as adults. As children, we felt wounded by parents who were too close or too far away. Now, as adults, we feel wounded by unempowering social roles and expectations that do not support our innate intelligence and creativity. We are sad, many of us, because we haven't explored our dreams or actualized our full potential.

Our families are victims of the economic and social pressures of an un-ideal world. Our children are victims of the mental/emotional demands of un-ideal parents. And so on it goes. I would venture to say it was not that different for my parents or theirs.

We who are in mourning cannot afford to add

to our burden of guilt. Yes, our parents made mistakes with us, and yes we do make the same or compensatory mistakes in bringing up our own children. Yes, there are emotional damages. I do not know of anyone who grew up without wounds. I know I did. I know that my son and daughter will have their own wounds to heal. I believe that is part of the process of being here. We need to make mistakes and learn from them.

Yes, I yearn for a perfect world. I yearn to be able to express my inner perfection all the time. But the truth is that I am not able to. To set perfection as my goal is suicidal. I am bound to fail, and blame myself.

Viewing myself as damaged goods because of what happened to me in the past is not empowering unless at some point I can heal my old emotional wounds. Viewing my children as damaged goods because they are the victims of my own "unhealed" child is not empowering either, unless I can forgive my mistakes and reach out to my children with greater patience and understanding.

If I have been wounded, it is because I needed to learn to heal. Let me take responsibility for that. Let me take responsibility for finding the place in me which is loved completely and cannot be manipulated or judged by others. If that place is not there, then I shall remain the victim of all my transgressions and all those that have been made against me.

I do not believe that it helps me to be the victim. Even, as a child, I chose my reality. I chose my lessons. My life is mine and no one can take it away from me. No matter how painful my life has been, nobody can say that I should have had a different life. If I had a different life, I would not have learned the lessons I needed to learn. I realize that this is not any easy statement to accept. What about all those victims of concentration camps? What about those children who starved to death in Ethiopia? What about all the victims of abuse? Were they not innocent? I say, "do not be so presumptuous as to judge the meaning of their lives."

Jesus was crucified, yet no one suggests that he should not have come to earth. Every life has a most profound meaning and is holy to the one who lives it.

I think it is time that we own our lives and forgive those we hold responsible for our wounds, including ourselves. I know that this is not easy. I know it is often a life-long process. But forgiveness is the cornerstone of the healing process, and we should not forget that.

Bradshaw is right, I think, in saying that it is an act of empowerment to "name the wound." It may also be an act of empowerment to "confront the offender." Every person must make that essential act of self-affirmation: "I have the right to exist as I am, and no one has the right to deny me this." The existential rights of every person are "inalienble," as our founding fathers proclaimed.

In talking about our wounds, we raise our consciousness. We understand the rights of the child in the same way that we understand the rights of women or minorities. We understand that these rights must be honored and protected. All this is positive. We look to the ideal. We seek to make the ideal manifest in our lives. But we also realize that we are not always able to measure up to our own expectations or the expectations of others. We need to learn to have more realistic expectations so that we do not punish ourselves unnecessarily.

Self-judgment is self-crucifixion. It does not

matter if I judge my present or my past, my adult or my child. Judgment wounds. It cannot empower.

Learning to love myself means learning to accept myself as I am, with all my wounds. That doesn't mean that I am not making an effort to heal those wounds. It means that every time I accept myself I am bringing healing to the hurt child within. Present healing may address past wounds, but healing happens in the present, not in the past.

While the child has the ability to heal herself, she will not use it until she feels loved and accepted. Until love is brought to the wounded child, she will use every piece of information to make the adult pay for her mistakes. Guilt is one of her favorite weapons. She can't help it. "I'm unhappy, so I'll make you unhappy too," is her battlecry.

I have said before that the ego of the wounded child is arrested in its development. Its demands for love and attention are always unreasonable. Not having received love without strings attached, the child does not know how to ask for love simply and directly.

When the child begins to feel loved and accepted, he also starts to perceive a reality that is larger than his survival needs. Gradually he learns to trust others and to stop manipulating people to get his needs met. Instead of using guilt as a tool to keep people in place in his emotional life, he learns to let go and accept the love that people offer to him freely.

In this way, the child enters the circle of atonement. She learns to give love as she would receive it, free of bargains and conditions. She learns to join with others as an equal who needs to give and receive, lead and follow, teach and learn. In this way, adult and child are healed together.

This is a lifelong healing process in which everyone makes mistakes and everyone asks for forgiveness. In this process, every moment, every interaction, is a healing moment, regardless of the number of mistakes that are made. It is a process in which we stop trying to love ourselves as we "should be" and start loving ourselves as we are.

I believe this is the essence of inner child work. It takes us through our fear, our guilt and our feelings of separation into the circle of love and acceptance. There we stay, not through any great achievement, but simply by being willing to forgive ourselves and each other whenever necessary. Whenever we appear to be in conflict or think that our needs are not being met, we know that the child within is not feeling loved. And then we turn to her and bless her and thank her. And then we reach out to others and ask for their support and their love.

A COURSE IN MIRACLES says that all attack, and all perception of lack is just a call for love. For years, we tried to live without love. We pretended we didn't need it. We put on a good show, but a show it was. Our pain bled through the masks we wore. Our self hatred wrote its legacy on the faces of our children. We finally had to come to grips with the fact that our charade of denial had failed.

Now we know that we hurt and we know that we need love. It is a great place to be. It is a place where we can be vulnerable and reach out to each other. Now we can be healthy children, willing to learn, willing to grow up and take responsibility for our lives. I am convinced that when our healing process is complete, the world will be a very different place than it was when we began.

LOVE WITHOUT CONDITIONS

Wounds deform the body/mind. Love expands its boundaries.

All who attack do so out of fear. They see attack as their escape from fear. Yet attack makes them feel guilty. And the more guilty they feel, the more they expect to be attacked and the more fearful they become. It is a vicious cycle.

There are no short-cuts out of separation and fear. These are states that indicate a lack of love. The only way to cross over these troubled waters is to ask for love and to be willing to give and receive it. Anything else is just denial. Anything else just deepens the pain of separation.

The idea that attack will take us out of fear is preposterous. The idea that blaming others (a form of attack) will remove our discomfort is ludicrous.

Our psychological state is simple, before we convolute it by giving ourselves permission to attack or defend. We don't feel loved and we want to feel loved. There is nothing mysterious about this feeling. We all have it. We had it as children. We have it as adults.

In this world, loving is a two way street. We tend to respond lovingly to those who offer us love, and defensively to those who attack us or withdraw from us. If we don't feel loved, it is usually because we're not being very loving to others or receptive to their expressions of love.

Many of us push love away because we are afraid of it. If we say "don't touch me" most people won't, because they don't hear this as a call for love. Only a person who is not ego-involved with us can see through our defenses and offer us the love we want, but for which we are afraid to ask.

Why are we so afraid to ask for what we want? Such a simple request would make life easier and more enjoyable for all of us. When we feel unloved, why can't we ask for love instead of attacking or running away?

Asking for love undoes the vicious cycle and makes us directly responsible for our healing process. When we ask for love and receive it, we no longer have any excuse why we can't reach out to others in kind. When we ask for love and don't receive it, we have to learn to love ourselves through our pain. Many of us are not ready to own this responsibility. We would rather project it onto someone else.

We step into our own suffering by refusing to take responsibility for our need for love. Although the need for love is universal, we are still ashamed to ask for it. We think that asking for love means we are weak and unloveable. If we have ever asked for love and been rejected, we are often unwilling to ask again. We think that we are the only ones who need love, that everyone else already has it. This is how separate we feel.

It is difficult for me to say to you: "I am lonely. I am afraid. I need your love and support." I would rather make you feel guilty, so that you will pay attention to me without my having to ask you directly. That way I can control you.

Control really is a major piece behind our feelings of fear and separation. If I have withdrawn from you, I want you to love me without making any demands on me. I want you to love me in a way that feels safe to me, that does not threaten my defenses. The idea that I can receive your love however you choose to give it is foreign to me. I don't trust myself to love in that way. And I don't trust you either.

I would rather go without love than receive it

on your terms. I see your love as an attack on me. In other words, it is inconceivable to me that you could love me unconditionally. I see your love of me as a way that you get your needs met, not as a way that I can get mine met.

The only way I can get my needs met, I think, is by controlling the way you love me. If you won't let me control the way you love me, then I will reject your love outright. I will pretend that I don't need it.

You see how complicated all this gets. We need love but we don't trust anyone else to give it without lots of strings attached. So we manipulate to get the love we want, yet we are never satisfied with what comes back. That is because people who allow us to control their love are not really loving us. They are responding to demands. And, even though this is what we supposedly want, it does not meet our deep seated need for unconditional love and acceptance.

Deep down inside we know the difference between love that responds to demands and love that is freely given. One is predictable but without nourishment. The other energizes but is unpredictable.

What a dilemma! This idea of love is not as easy as we think. No matter how hard we try, we cannot control love. Our willingness to be loved means that we trust the person who wants to love us and we feel that the environment surrounding that love is supportive.

If we choose relationships with people we fail to trust or environments for love which are too volatile or restrictive, then we can be sure that we are still asking for love with inappropriate conditions. "I can receive love only from a person who loves me intensely but cannot commit to me, or only from a person who commits but doesn't make emotional demands on me." Does that sound familiar?

Anyone who has been in a relationship with a married woman or married man knows the first scenario. The married man or woman often knows both scenarios, the first with a lover, and the second with a mate.

Trusting the other person to love us without preconditions in an environment we can't control requires a leap of faith. Yes, it means faith in the other person. It means faith in the universe. But, most of all, it means faith in ourselves.

It means that I can love you without guarantees that you will stay back or that you will stay close. It indicates that I can receive your love as you give it without judging it as too little or as too much. It suggests that I can be grateful for your love, but not dependent on it, that your love can challenge me to grow and accept myself more fully and mine can do the same for you.

This is the kind of love that nurtures and inspires us. It is love that comes to us because we are willing to face our fears and gradually let down our defenses. It is a mature love, a love amongst equals, a love that supports mutuality.

I cannot come to this love so long as I am afraid of it. And I will be afraid of it until I am willing to leave my neurotic need for control behind. Beneath that need to control, and all the complex, often contradictory behaviors associated with it, is a deep-seated belief in my separation from others. Every opportunity to love or be loved challenges that belief and helps me overcome it, if only I am willing to share who I am with my partner.

Lest my partner comes to know me as I am and vice versa, we cannot meet on the high ground of truth. Instead we take the muddy road of co-dependency in which each seeks in vain to control the other's love, a process which we both unconsciously resist because it is incompatible with our spiritual needs.

❂

SEPARATION AND ATONEMENT

Grace comes when we live a life based on trust instead of control. It is the fruit of our willingness to join the Circle of Atonement.

Separation, or the movement away from God, is the attempt to find an isolated, exclusive purpose on our journey. As long as our purpose is held up against that of others for comparison and judgment, it continues to serve the Separation. It evokes fear and creates division between us, as well as within our own psyches.

The message of the Atonement is that no purpose can be satisfying until it is shared with others. Then, it ceases to be our exclusive possession, and becomes a creation of our love.

The Atonement is the answer to the Separation. It is the movement back toward God. Its process is love, just as the process of the Separation is fear.

We have seen the world that fear makes. We don't like that world inside us or as it is reflected outside. The creations of fear — suspicion, envy, judgment, mistrust, perceived inequality, etc.— wound us and confuse us. They make it impossible for us to meet in our innocence or see face to face.

By contrast, the creations of love — trust, joy, enthusiasm, faith, perceived equality and so on — empower us to live our truth and enable us to support others in doing the same. The Atonement is a time when we recognize our common wounds and our common need for healing. It is a time when we know that we need each other as helpmates and teachers. It is a time when we make a conscious decision, individually and collectively, not to be ruled by our fears any longer.

The movement back to God does not happen all at once for most of us. It is a process of learning to trust ourselves and others. It is a process of learning to live without setting conditions, without manipulating. It is a process in which we learn not to carry the past and to be open and optimistic about the future.

Because we have joined the circle of love does not mean that fear does not come up for us any more. It means that we have made the choice to walk through fear to love. It does not mean that we no longer feel separate from one another. It means that we have made the decision to cross over the artificial boundaries we place between us.

The Atonement begins midway in the cycle of manifestation. Separation has peaked and begun to subside. Joining begins. We are still a long way away from total trust in ourselves and each other, but we have begun the movement back to God. It is the beginning of our conscious journey toward love and acceptance. Progress may be slow but we can see it. Regression may occur, but it is temporary and we know it. Even when we lose our confidence, we know that sooner or later we will regain it. We trust our process, however tentative it seems. We move forward step by step.

Those who have gone through Twelve Step Programs know the importance of steady, determined progress. But the twelve steps are only the beginning. There are hundreds, perhaps thousands of steps back to God. That is okay. We still need to take one step at a time. And we need to know that in taking that step, we are taking all of the others as well. Every expression of love is maximal. The whole process of Atonement is present here and now.

The journey home is just a metaphor for a process that begins and ends in our own hearts and minds. A COURSE IN MIRACLES calls it "a journey without distance to a goal that has never changed." We begin with love and end with it. Love is what we are: all of us are just different sizes and shapes of love made manifest. But we get hung up on our differences. We separate from each other and feel anxious and disoriented when we do so. We can't help but experience fear whenever we disconnect ourselves from the Source of love. Our attack on each other is just a symptom of our separation anxiety. Meanwhile, our connection with one another remains beneath the surface. Our separateness is an illusion, but it continues to block our access to love as long as we think it is real.

We do not awaken from the illusion until we see how it abuses us. Our journey in the body, in the world, is nothing more or less than a process of awakening to a love that never left us. Our dream of attack is but a dream. It seems to take casualties, but those wounds are healed in the instant of awakening. It seems to cut us off from those we love, but now we see them at our side. Indeed nothing has been gained nor lost. We have simply returned home. It is a familiar place, a place where we are comfortable with ourselves and each other. We wonder why we left it in the first place.

Why would we choose to be born and die if we live eternally in the circle of love? Why would we stray from the body of truth, the heart of grace? It just does not make sense. Or does it? It would be foolish of me to pretend to know any more than you do. Yet somehow I believe that our lives themselves are the answer.

Part Nine

Miracles and Grace

WHAT IS A MIRACLE?

When I first heard the title A COURSE IN MIRACLES, I assumed it was some kind of half-baked born-again Christian crusade. "How could anyone take miracles seriously?" I wondered. Surely these people must know that miracles are to be read symbolically, not literally. The idea that someone could interpret miracles literally was, to me, naive.

Later, when I began to study The Course, I realized that the definition of "miracle" was quite different from what I expected. The Course talked about the miracle as a change in perception, a different way of seeing the world, a way of looking based on love instead of fear. That psychological definition was easier for me to understand and accept.

It meant that if I changed the way I perceived events, I would be changing the meaning of events. And if I could change what an event meant to me, I was literally transforming that event. Changes in thinking meant changes in reality.

The cause of my happiness or unhappiness was thus to be found not in what happened to me, but in the interpretation I placed on it. Things could happen in my life which others could view as horrible, yet to me they could be a blessing if I brought the right attitude to them.

When the real estate market collapsed and I lost all the money I had made over a ten year period, it seemed a terrible blow. Others in my position lost not only their money, but the emotional support of family and friends. I was not so unfortunate. For me, the event was a test of my ability to stay positive under adverse conditions. It also gave me permission to shift my focus from doing real estate, which I did not enjoy, to writing and teaching, which I did enjoy.

I know others who have been able to use the shocking energy of a life threatening illness or death of a loved-one to motivate them to heal themselves and minister to others less fortunate then them. It is extraordinary to realize that under conditions that are wounding to some people, others are able to rise to their greatest heights.

How do we explain this? Some people are born in the ghetto, yet become great dancers or musicians. Adversity affects people differently. In some it builds character. In others, it brings out self-pity.

By contrast, some people who are born with greatest resources available to them become drug addicts or commit suicide. Obviously material wealth does not by itself bring happiness. Even emotional support does not guarantee that a person will flourish. Some people grow up with lots of love and support, yet never learn to love themselves. Now one might say that such people are the exception. And I agree. But people who heal themselves of cancer are also the exception! Both show the extraordinary power of the mind to make things better or worse than they seem to be.

Don't get me wrong. I think that everyone should have enough to eat, a decent place to live, a good education, and lot's of love and support. That is what we deserve. That will help us to actualize our potential. But it will not guarantee self-actualization, because that is something we affirm or deny within.

Receiving love makes it easier for us to learn to love ourselves and others, but it does not guarantee it. We can do everything right and still feel wrong. We are not Pavlovian mice shaped only by stimulus/response, by external rewards and punishments. We are beings with consciousness. We have predispositions and beliefs about ourselves that determine "how" we experience, if not "what" we experience as well.

RE-INCARNATION AND THE
MYTH OF TIME

My childhood was not particularly traumatic in external terms, although it felt traumatic to me. My parents did the best they could. They were nice people who were scared and frustrated and I'm sure I learned some of my negative patterns from them, as they learned theirs from their folks. But at every step along the way, I chose how I would interpret the input I received.

All through our lives we are making choices. In romanticizing the concept of childhood, we tend to look at children as blank slates that simply get filled up as children imitate their role models. I don't say that this is untrue. I just say it's not completely true. Children are not blank slates. No conscious being is a blank slate.

It is fairly well accepted that we come into the body with a genetic imprint. That imprint does not just manifest in physical terms, but also in psychological terms. We may be predisposed to develop certain beliefs, just as we are predisposed to develop certain physical conditions.

Eastern religions talk a lot about these predispositions, which they call karmas, or samskaras. Some people simply act out their predispositions. Others can alter them by bringing awareness to their tendencies and choosing a different response to life.

A COURSE IN MIRACLES is considered a course in mind training. It seeks to correct the false beliefs or "illusions" which predispose us to creating pain and suffering in our lives.

The profound understandings of The Course are relevant whether or not you believe in reincarnation. If you do, you probably think that you chose your parents. If you don't, you probably think that you had no choice in the matter. But, even if you did not choose your parents, you must concede that you do have a choice in how you react to your parent's influence.

Perhaps you believe that you are not responsible for your childhood. That was a time when things were "done" to you. Your reactions were automatic. Anyone would have reacted that way. Well, even if you are right, you are an adult now, and you do have choices. You are responsible.

We don't have to talk about the past. The key is whether or not we are willing to acknowledge and take responsibility in the present.

The concept of life before birth just places the responsibility earlier on in the process. It says the child was attracted to certain parents because of who he is. You can reject that idea, and place responsibility from birth onward, or from age 6 or age 18. It doesn't really matter so long as you feel you are responsible now. The rest is just theory. It doesn't help, and if you get too deeply involved in it, it can actually hold you back, because it will preoccupy you and keep you from finding the point of power in your life, which is the present.

You can deny "choice" in every moment of your life up till now, and still learn to take responsibility for what you are going to create now. Even if you refuse to take responsibility in this moment, you can decide to in the next.

"Choose again," The Course tells us. You simply made a mistake. You need to see that your assumptions are incorrect. Incorrect assumptions lead to events that are not supportive to your personhood.

You can make a different choice. You can learn

from your mistakes. You can see things differently. Because you feel pain in your life now does not mean the pain needs to continue.

There is never a time in your life when you cannot step closer to God if you want to. Every time you turn a negative perception into a positive one, you move more deeply into love's embrace. Your "little willingness" to change your mind contains the seeds for the greatest miracles.

The Course says "there is no order of difficulty in miracles." One is not harder or easier than another. Every miracle represents a change in perception. Even the events and circumstances in your life which seem fixed in stone are subject to transformation by changing the beliefs which hold them in place.

FORGIVENESS

As The Course says, one of the greatest of all miracles is the one that changes "an ancient hatred" to a "present love." We all have misperceptions and misunderstandings in our lives. We all have people we have rejected, people we have cast out of our hearts, perhaps for a few days or weeks, perhaps for many years. No matter how we may justify our actions, our lives are not as rich without the presence of these people.

I remember a lesbian couple my wife and I were close to. I felt great love for these two people, and I had invited them to join in one of my meditation and healing groups. Yet in spite of my love for them, I could not fully accept their lifestyle. I felt okay about their relationship, because it clearly was a loving one. But when they politicized it by saying that being bisexual was more honest and natural than being heterosexual, I had a hard time. In retrospect, I can see that their need to make such statements was a direct response to feeling threatened by my subtle judgment of them. They felt my attack and attacked back.

One Christmas day, we invited them over to eat with us. We were having a great time, when the conversation somehow changed to lesbian and gay issues. They made some statements that I found hard to accept and I challenged them. The more we disagreed, the more personal the conversation seemed to become until we were all feeling somewhat hurt and defensive. We tried to put a good face on things before they left, but I could feel that they left wounded.

In spite of many attempts on our part to heal the situation, our friends chose to hold onto their wounds. They withdrew from us emotionally, became inaccessible and suspicious of any attempts at reconciliation.

Initially, I felt depressed whenever I thought about them. I had to discipline my mind so that I would think positive thoughts about them. I spent months working on forgiveness, forgiveness of myself for judging them, and forgiveness of them for judging me.

As Christmas approaches this year, I can't help but remember the talk in the living room and the feelings of betrayal. It is so ironic that such a negative event happened on Christmas day. The significance of that was not lost on me when it happened and it isn't now. For me, it was a major lesson.

I still love my friends and I miss them. My life is not as full without their presence. As I overcome my own judgments, I hope that they will overcome theirs so that we can meet once again with trust in our hearts. I believe that our lives will be more complete when we stop pushing each other away.

We all have someone to forgive, someone we have cast out of our hearts and out of our lives. It may be difficult to bring this person back into the circle of love, but it is not impossible. If we do not try, we are allowing ourselves to shrink emotionally.

This Christmas, let us remember that the circle of love must be extended if we are to feel love's presence within. That means doing what is difficult. It means going beyond the boundaries we have erected in fear.

❂

THE MEANING OF INNOCENCE

Jesus was innocent, yet he was crucified. Despite the unfair treatment he received, he did not condemn his attackers, but forgave them. Even on the cross, he chose love.

This was his witness to us, the teaching he lived with his life, his eternal legacy. Every year when Christmas comes, we have a choice. We can remember his death or his life, the attack against him or his forgiveness of it.

Many of us have had to stand up for what we believe in and suffer the consequences. Whenever we oppose the institutions of society, however exploitative they are, we must pay the price. We are isolated, ridiculed and attacked. It is no different today than it was in Jesus' time.

And it is just as important to stand up for truth today as it was then. This often means that we must take an unpopular position which is threatening to others because it challenges their values. Guilt runs so deep in everybody's psyche, it does not take much to offend someone.

People who hold spiritual values often threaten the status quo. Society is always trying to manipulate spiritual values. Social values are the lowest common denominator. They represent the minimum moral standard people are willing to accept. To be sure, this minimum differs from country to country, but it is always lower than the values advocated by the spiritual teachers in those places.

The commandment "thou shalt not kill" becomes "thou shalt not kill unless someone attacks you" and "love your neighbor" becomes "love your neighbor as long as he is nice to you." It is easy to secularize the word of God. You just move it from the absolute to the relative, from the unconditional to the conditional.

Jesus did not tolerate such tomfoolery. Nor did he tolerate spiritual practices performed by rote. He spoke to the spirit of the law and looked for that spirit to be embodied in the act of worship. That is why he was such a great teacher. He insisted that spirituality be integrated into daily life.

"Love your enemies," he said. Everyone deserves love, even the people you cast out of your heart. Anyone can love their friends. That is not so hard. But only one who walks a spiritual path tries to love his enemies.

We are all working on the same universal lessons. That is clear. Yet, equally clear is the fact that we are all in different places on the journey. To compare where we are is foolish. No one is really ahead or behind. It only seems that way.

I am not responsible to be where you are, nor are you responsible to be where I am. That seems like such a simple thing. But it's not. We can't stop comparing. I think what works for me should work for you, and you think what works for you should work for me. It's just not true.

My son feeds his fish stuff I wouldn't dream of eating. I don't think they'd like to eat what I eat either. We all eat what tastes good to us. And what tastes good to me often tastes very bad to you. We need to get used to this. We can't stay on our own path, if we don't have tolerance for the views of others.

My innocence lies in my ability to be without judging. If I learn from my mistakes, I won't carry guilt around. And if I don't carry guilt, I won't need to judge you. It is really that simple.

The teaching is not conceptually difficult. It is

demanding in other ways. It insists that there be no dichotomy between what I believe and how I live. That cuts through all the justifications, elaborate defense systems, and illusory beliefs. It streamlines spirituality and makes it possible to practice day by day, hour by hour.

If I believe in love, my goal is to love not just the people I like, but every person I encounter. If I can't do that, my belief is not fully integrated in my life. I need more practice. I need a few more lessons to show me what I have to work on.

My innocence is wrapped in all kinds of judgments about myself and you. Yours is wrapped in similar clothes. Perhaps your clothes are a little different from mine, but so what? We can spend a whole lifetime comparing what we are wearing without getting down to the essence of it all. Beneath all these clothes, we both are naked. Beneath all these judgments is your innocence and mine.

By constantly choosing love over fear, Jesus was able to reflect back to us our innocence. He enabled us to see ourselves, not through the judgmental eyes of society, but as God sees us. And he asked us to look upon each other in the same way. I don't say that is easy to do. To be sure, I struggle with this as much as you do. I believe that is why we are here. The first coming saw the embodiment of the teaching in a single man's life. The second coming will see the teaching embodied in all of our lives. That is also called the Atonement.

When I see your innocence and you see mine, we bless and bring each other into the circle of love. This circle has no limits except the ones we impose on it, and those boundaries arise out of fear. They are illusory boundaries, yet they keep us in chains as long as we hold onto judgment and guilt.

Jesus and other great teachers have shown us a way out of that dilemma. Yet each of us must embrace that way when he or she is ready. There can be no forcing of truth.

A COURSE IN MIRACLES says that we can't choose the curriculum, but we can decide when to take it. I think that is very accurate. That is why the message of Jesus is as important today as it was 2,000 years ago. Some of us are just enrolling in class, and the rest of us have been taking lessons only for a short time!

✹

TRUST AND GRACE

Whenever I am asked to look at myself more deeply and see my transgressions, it is difficult. Whenever I am asked to embrace someone who has attacked me, it is difficult. Whenever I am asked to heal old wounds and expand my emotional boundaries, it is hard for me. How can I expect it to be otherwise?

If it were easy to grow, we would all do it and be done with it. But it is not so easy. Every time I make someone wrong, I must confront that judgment inwardly. Every limitation I place on my brother or sister, I must cross over in my own mind.

In the heat of the moment, my attack always feels justified, but it never is. I remember one time I was talking with my uncle on my brother's porch. He was going on and on about some guy who was helping him collect his poems, and how lucky he was to have this guy help him, and how it was only a matter of time before his work was accepted. Listening to my uncle, I felt he was deluding himself. His work was difficult for people to understand. That's why it wasn't popular. And this guy who was helping him, what did he do? He gave my uncle a university label to put on his books, but my uncle still had to come up with the money to print them. What was so generous about that?

I could have kept these thoughts to myself, but I didn't. I attacked. I didn't even know I was attacking. I thought I was protecting my uncle from another disappointment. But I was wrong. He was hurt by what I said. It brought up old wounds, wounds I didn't even know existed.

I was aghast as I listened to my uncle spout out

examples of unkind things I had said to him 20 years ago. He was still hanging onto every negative word I ever said to him. These memories were so vivid, it was as though he was looking at me through them. My present attack was just the straw that broke the camel's back. Moreover, he didn't seem to remember any of the positive things, which indeed predominated in our relationship, as I was devoted to him for many years.

I was amazed, but there on the porch I had to confront the fact that I had said things, which true or not, injured my uncle and took a negative toll on our relationship. I was responsible for my actions. I had to witness to their affect on another human being.

No, I did not blame myself or him. I was grateful for this moment. Tense though it was, it was also telling. It was a moment in which all of the buried pain of the past surfaced so that it could be seen and dealt with. It was unsettling, but it had a positive effect on me, because it forced me to look more deeply at myself.

A couple of days later, on Easter morning, I wrote a poem for my uncle about forgiveness. It was an olive branch, and he seemed to accept it. It was the beginning of a healing process that has continued, however slowly. It is not easy to heal old wounds, but they must be healed or they hold us hostage to the past.

I know that I am not the only man my uncle has gotten close to. There were three men before me who loved him deeply. Yet all three had to separate from him to be faithful to themselves. My uncle was a strong presence in their lives, a presence that supported their creativity as long as they accepted his work and his behavior uncritically. In all cases, that arrangement could not continue indefinitely. When separation came, it was often bitter.

So I know that all of the stuff that came out on the porch did not belong to me. But some of it did. And that is the piece I had to own.

When I was in my late teens and early twenties, I reached a point in my relationship with my uncle when I could no longer accept him uncritically. I could no longer try to live my creative life through his. I could no longer be 90% his advocate and 10% my own. I needed space. I needed to live my own life, evolve my own art. I always thought he understood.

In a way he did. But it is hard to give up the unconditional praise and admiration of a younger person, even if you know it is a developmental necessity for him. The relationship begins to change. Giving and receiving take different forms, different percentages perhaps. I can understand my uncle's difficulty. No matter how much you try to let go, ego needs get in the way. There are moments of attack and counterattack.

My uncle remembered these moments, but not the context around them. That's okay. I really needed to know that he was holding these old wounds. I could not begin to address them until I knew they were there.

It always amazes me that when the balance of power in a relationship begins to change, the situation often gets messy. It doesn't matter if this happens between parent and child, between spouses, or between significant others, since parent- child dynamics get played out in most intimate relationships.

It is the nature of life for children to grow up and find their own way. That doesn't make it any

easier for the parent or for the child when this time
of separation comes. All one can do is try to honor
the adolescent's need for independence separation
with the same integrity that one tried to honor the
young infant child's need for bonding.

Was my attack on my uncle on the porch an
assertion of my power and independence. Yes, probably. Was it necessary? Probably not.

Letting go is the hardest thing we are asked to
do. We come close to each other. We become dependent on one another. We see our lives constantly
in relationship to each other, in positive and negative ways. There is plenty of pushing and shoving,
as well as plenty of support. And then, often without
a whole lot of warning, we are asked to let go.

Children grow up. Parents die. Old friends and
lovers disappear from our lives. The nature of intimacy changes. Increasingly, we learn to rely on more
subtle, non-physical demonstrations of love. We
experience our aloneness in a different way. Friendship becomes the most reliable bond in our lives. We
do not struggle so hard to gain the upper hand in
our relationships, because we see our equality earlier
on. We don't need as much from each other as we
did when we were young.

We look out and see each other's beauty, each
other's fragility. And we know that one day the other
person will breathe their last breath and we will see
them no more. And we know that one day we too
will breathe our last breath and we will not be the
same. Something will change, just as something has
changed each time we moved into a different stage
of our lives. Something will change and it will be
okay. It won't be easy perhaps. It rarely is.

Or perhaps this one time, it will be easy. Perhaps

this one time, letting go will not be a leaving behind, but a joining. Perhaps this one time we will not be afraid, but we will feel the love of God in our hearts as we go. And we will enter that warmth and that light without judgment or fear.

I trust that it will be that way for us. May we trust God to guide us to the door when we are ready to open it. That will be the end of one moment of our eternal journey, one moment in time joining the timeless, one embodiment of love returning to love's embrace.

Namaste, Paul Ferrini
Christmas, 1990

P aul Ferrini is the author of numerous books which help us heal the emotional body and embrace a spirituality grounded in the real challenges of daily life. Paul's work is heart-centered and experiential, empowering us to move through our fear and shame and share who we are authentically with others. Paul Ferrini founded and edited *Miracles Magazine*, a publication devoted to telling Miracle Stories offering hope and inspiration to all of us. Paul's conferences, retreats and *Affinity Group Process* have helped thousands of people deepen their practice of forgiveness and open their hearts to the Divine presence in themselves and others. For more information on Paul's workshops and retreats or *The Affinity Group Process*, contact Heartways Press, P.O. Box 181, South Deerfield, MA 01373 or call 413-665-0555.

═══ New From Heartways Press ═══
and Paul Ferrini

Volume III of The Christ Mind Series is Hot Off the Press!

"The most important books I have read. I study them like a Bible."
— Elisabeth Kübler-Ross, M.D.

"Paul Ferrini is a modern-day Kahlil Gibran — poet, mystic, visionary, teller of truth."
— Larry Dossey, M.D.

Miracle of Love
Reflections of the
Christ Mind,
Part III
by Paul Ferrini

ISBN 1-879159-23-6
$12.95
192 pages, paperback

Many people say that this latest volume of the Christ Mind series is the best yet. Jesus tells us:"I was born to a simple woman in a barn. She was no more a virgin than your mother was." Moreover, he tells us, the virgin birth is not the only myth surrounding his life and teaching. So are the concepts of vicarious atonement and physical resurrection. Relentlessly, the master tears down the rigid dogma and hierarchical teachings that obscure his simple message of love and forgiveness. He encourages us to take him down from the pedestal and the cross and see him as an equal brother who found the way out of suffering by opening his heart totally. We too can open our hearts and find peace and happiness. "The power of love will make miracles in your life as wonderful as any attributed to me," he tells us. "Your birth into this embodiment is no less holy than mine. The love that you extend to others is no less important than the love I extend to you."

A Poetic Exploration of Healing and Forgiveness

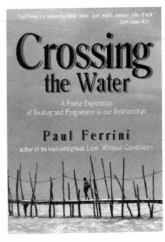

Crossing The Water:
A Poetic Exploration
of Healing
and Forgiveness
in Our Relationships
by Paul Ferrini

ISBN 1-879159-25-2
$9.95
96 pages, paperback

Part One, *The Elegy of the Stones*, is an epic poem about ego-resistance and surrender in an intimate relationship. Using the imagery of the river, Ferrini shows how the rough edges of our personalities are worn smooth in the context of a committed relationship just as the rocks in the river are "pounded and caressed to rounded stone." Part Two, *The Fountainhead*, explores the importance of staying in the present moment and facing the fears that come up in our relationships. Ferrini writes *In this lifetime, /what we are afraid of /comes to look at us /in the eyes.* If we want to experience intimacy, we must cross the water of our own emotional pain and open *that frozen passage way in the heart /where the stream begins.* Part Three, *The Certainty of the Leaves*, features an Elegy for Stephen Camp, a talented musician and close friend of the author, who opened his heart to love and forgiveness before dying of a brain tumor in 1996. In the end, even death becomes an act of "crossing the water," moving from pain to joy, from fear to love, and from separation to oneness.

Now Finally our Bestselling Title on Audio Tape

Love Without Conditions,
Reflections
of the Christ Mind, Part I
by Paul Ferrini

The Book on Tape
Read by the Author
2 Cassettes,
Approximately 3.25 hours

ISBN 1-879159-24-4
$19.95

Now on audio tape: the incredible book from Jesus calling us to awaken to our own Christhood. Listen to this gentle, profound, book while driving in your car or before going to sleep at night. Elisabeth Kubler-Ross calls this "the most important book I have read. I study it like a Bible." Find out for yourself how this amazing book has helped thousands of people understand the radical teachings of the master and begin to integrate these teachings into their lives.

Risen Christ Posters and Notecards

11"x17" Poster
suitable for framing
ISBN 1-879159-19-8 $10.00

Set of 8 Notecards
with Envelopes
ISBN 1-879159-20-1 $10.00

Ecstatic Moment Posters and Notecards

8.5"x11" Poster
suitable for framing
ISBN 1-879159-21-X $5.00

Set of 8 Notecards
with Envelopes
ISBN 1-879159-22-8 $10.00

══ Heartways Press ══

"Integrating Spirituality into Daily Life"
More Books by Paul Ferrini

• Waking Up Together
Illuminations on the Road
to Nowhere

There comes a time for all of us when the outer destinations no longer satisfy and we finally understand that the love and happiness we seek cannot be found outside of us. It must be found in our own hearts, on the other side of our pain. "The Road to Nowhere is the path through your heart. It is not a journey of escape. It is a journey through your pain to end the pain of separation."

This book makes it clear that we can no longer rely on outer teachers or teachings to find our spiritual identity. Nor can we find who we are in relationships where boundaries are blurred and one person makes decisions for another. If we want to be authentic, we can't allow anyone else to be an authority for us, nor can we allow ourselves to be an authority for another person.

Authentic relationships happen between equal partners who take responsibility for their own consciousness and experience. When their buttons are pushed, they are willing to look at the obstacles they have erected to the experience of love and acceptance. As they understand and surrender the false ideas and emotional reactions that create separation, genuine intimacy becomes possible, and the sacred dimension of the relationship is born. 216 pp. paper ISBN 1-879159-17-1 $14.95

230

• The Ecstatic Moment:
A Practical Manual for Opening Your Heart and Staying in It.

A simple, power-packed guide that helps us take appropriate responsibility for our experience and establish healthy boundaries with others. Part II contains many helpful exercises and meditations that teach us to stay centered, clear and open in heart and mind. The Affinity Group Process and other group practices help us learn important listening and communication skills that can transform our troubled relationships. Once you have read this book, you will keep it in your briefcase or on your bedside table, referring to it often. You will not find a more practical, down to earth guide to contemporary spirituality. You will want to order copies for all your friends. 128 pp. paper ISBN 1-879159-18-X $10.95

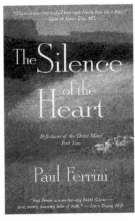

• The Silence of the Heart
Reflections of the Christ Mind,
Part Two

A powerful sequel to *Love Without Conditions*. John Bradshaw says: "with deep insight and sparkling clarity, this book demonstrates that the roots of all abuse are to be found in our own self-betrayal. Paul Ferrini leads us skillfully and courageously beyond shame, blame, and attachment to our wounds into the depths of self-forgiveness...a must read for all people who are ready to take responsibility for their own healing." 218 pp. paper.
ISBN 1-879159-16-3 $14.95

• Love Without Conditions:
Reflections of the Christ Mind - Part I
An incredible book from Jesus calling us to awaken to our Christhood. Rarely has any book conveyed the teachings of the master in such a simple but profound manner. This book will help you to bring your understanding from the head to the heart so that you can model the teachings of love and forgiveness in your daily life. 192 pp. paper ISBN 1-879159-15-15 $12.00

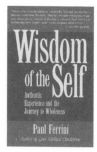

• The Wisdom of the Self
This ground-breaking book explores our authentic experience and our journey to wholeness. "Your life is your spiritual path. Don't be quick to abandon it for promises of bigger and better experiences. You are getting exactly the experiences you need to grow. If your growth seems too slow or uneventful for you, it is because you have not fully embraced the situations and relationships at hand...To know the Self is to allow everything, to embrace the totality of who we are, all that we think and feel, all of our fear, all of our love." 240 pp. paper ISBN 1-879159-14-7 $12.00

• The Twelve Steps of Forgiveness
A practical manual for healing ourselves and our relationships. This book gives us a step-by-step process for moving through our fears, projections, judgments, and guilt so that we can take responsibility for creating the life we want. With great gentleness, we learn to embrace our lessons and to find equality with others. A must read for all in recovery and others seeking spiritual wholeness. 144 pp. paper ISBN 1-879159-10-4 $10.00

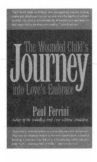

• The Wounded Child's Journey
Into Love's Embrace
This book explores a healing process in which
we confront our deep-seated guilt and fear,
bringing love and forgiveness to the wounded
child within. By surrendering our judgments of
self and others, we overcome feelings of separation and dismantle co-dependent patterns
that restrict our self-expression and ability to
give and receive love. 240pp. paper ISBN 1-
879159-06-6 $12.00

• The Bridge to Reality
A Heart-Centered Approach to *A Course in
Miracles* and the Process of Inner Healing.
Sharing his experiences of spiritual awakening, Paul emphasizes self-acceptance and
forgiveness as cornerstones of spiritual
practice. Presented with beautiful photos,
this book conveys the essence of *The
Course* as it is lived in daily life. 192 pp.
paper ISBN 1-879159-03-1 $12.00

• From Ego to Self
108 illustrated affirmations designed
to offer you a new way of viewing
conflict situations so that you can
overcome negative thinking and
bring more energy, faith and optimism into your life. 128 pp. paper
ISBN 1-879159-01-5 $10.00

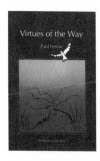

• Virtues of The Way

A lyrical work of contemporary scripture reminiscent of the Tao Te Ching. Beautifully illustrated, this inspirational book will help you cultivate the spiritual values required to fulfill your creative purpose and live in harmony with others. 64 pp. paper ISBN 1-879159-02-3 $7.50

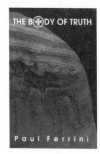

• The Body of Truth

A crystal clear introduction to the universal teachings of love and forgiveness. This book traces all forms of suffering to negative attitudes and false beliefs, which we have the ability to transform. 64 pp. paper ISBN 1-879159-02-3 $7.50

• Available Light

Inspirational, passionate poems dealing with the work of inner integration, love and relationships, death and re-birth, loss and abundance, life purpose and the reality of spiritual vision. 128 pp. paper ISBN 1-879159-05-8 $12.00

Guided Meditation Cassette Tapes
by Paul Ferrini

• **The Circle of Healing**
The meditation and healing tape that many of you have been seeking. This gentle meditation opens the heart to love's presence and extends that love to all the beings in your experience. A powerful tape with inspirational piano accompaniment by Michael Gray.
ISBN 1-879159-08-2 $10.00

• **Healing the Wounded Child**
A potent healing tape that accesses old feelings of pain, fragmentation, self-judgment and separation and brings them into the light of conscious awareness and acceptance. Side two includes a hauntingly beautiful "inner child" reading from *The Bridge to Reality* with piano accompaniment by Michael Gray.
ISBN 1-879159-11-2 $10.00

• **Forgiveness: Returning to the Original Blessing**
A self healing tape that helps us accept and learn from the mistakes we have made in the past. By letting go of our judgments and ending our ego-based search for perfection, we can bring our darkness to the light, dissolving anger, guilt, and shame. Piano accompaniment by Michael Gray.
ISBN 1-879159-12-0 $10.00

Heartways Press Order Form

Name_____

Address_____

City _____State _____Zip _____

Phone _____

BOOKS BY PAUL FERRINI

Miracle of Love ($12.95)
Crossing the Water ($9.95)   _____
Waking Up Together ($14.95)   _____
The Ecstatic Moment ($10.95)   _____
The Silence of the Heart ($14.95)   _____
Love Without Conditions ($12.00)   _____
The Wisdom of the Self ($12.00)   _____
The Twelve Steps of Forgiveness ($10.00)   _____
The Wounded Child's Journey into Love's Embrace ($12.00) _____
The Bridge to Reality ($12.00)   _____
From Ego to Self ($10.00)   _____
Virtues of the Way ($7.50)   _____
The Body of Truth ($7.50)   _____
Available Light ($10.00)   _____

AUDIO TAPES

Love Without Conditions ($19.95)
 (The book on tape read by the author)   _____
The Circle of Healing ($10.00)
Healing the Wounded Child ($10.00)   _____
Forgiveness: Returning to the Original Blessing ($10.00) _____

POSTERS AND NOTECARDS

Risen Christ Poster 11"x17" ($10.00)
Ecstatic Moment Poster 8.5"x11" ($5.00)   _____
Risen Christ Notecards with envelopes 8/pkg ($10.00)   _____
Ecstatic Moment Notecards with envelopes 8/pkg ($10.00) _____

SHIPPING

($2.00 for first item, $1.00 each additional item.
Add additional $1.00 for first class postage.)   _____
MA residents please add 5% sales tax.   _____

                                   TOTAL $_____

Send Order To: Heartways Press
P. O. Box 181, South Deerfield, MA 01373   Please allow
Toll free: 1-888-HARTWAY• 413-665-0555   1-2 weeks
                                                      for delivery

Heartways Press Order Form

Name_____

Address_____

City _____State _____Zip _____

Phone _____

BOOKS BY PAUL FERRINI

Miracle of Love ($12.95)
Crossing the Water ($9.95)   _____
Waking Up Together ($14.95)   _____
The Ecstatic Moment ($10.95)   _____
The Silence of the Heart ($14.95)   _____
Love Without Conditions ($12.00)   _____
The Wisdom of the Self ($12.00)   _____
The Twelve Steps of Forgiveness ($10.00)   _____
The Wounded Child's Journey into Love's Embrace ($12.00)   _____
The Bridge to Reality ($12.00)   _____
From Ego to Self ($10.00)   _____
Virtues of the Way ($7.50)   _____
The Body of Truth ($7.50)   _____
Available Light ($10.00)   _____

AUDIO TAPES

Love Without Conditions ($19.95)   _____
   (The book on tape read by the author)
The Circle of Healing ($10.00)   _____
Healing the Wounded Child ($10.00)   _____
Forgiveness: Returning to the Original Blessing ($10.00)   _____

POSTERS AND NOTECARDS

Risen Christ Poster 11"x17" ($10.00)
Ecstatic Moment Poster 8.5"x11" ($5.00)   _____
Risen Christ Notecards with envelopes 8/pkg ($10.00)   _____
Ecstatic Moment Notecards with envelopes 8/pkg ($10.00)   _____

SHIPPING

($2.00 for first item, $1.00 each additional item.
Add additional $1.00 for first class postage.)
MA residents please add 5% sales tax.   _____
                                                             _____

                                    TOTAL   **$_____**

Send Order To: Heartways Press
P. O. Box 181, South Deerfield, MA 01373   *Please allow*
Toll free: 1-888-HARTWAY• 413-665-0555   *1-2 weeks*
                                                for delivery

Heartways Press Order Form

Name_____

Address_____

City _____State _____Zip _____

Phone _____

BOOKS BY PAUL FERRINI

Miracle of Love ($12.95)   _____
Crossing the Water ($9.95)   _____
Waking Up Together ($14.95)   _____
The Ecstatic Moment ($10.95)   _____
The Silence of the Heart ($14.95)   _____
Love Without Conditions ($12.00)   _____
The Wisdom of the Self ($12.00)   _____
The Twelve Steps of Forgiveness ($10.00)   _____
The Wounded Child's Journey into Love's Embrace ($12.00)   _____
The Bridge to Reality ($12.00)   _____
From Ego to Self ($10.00)   _____
Virtues of the Way ($7.50)   _____
The Body of Truth ($7.50)   _____
Available Light ($10.00)   _____

AUDIO TAPES

Love Without Conditions ($19.95)   _____
  (The book on tape read by the author)
The Circle of Healing ($10.00)   _____
Healing the Wounded Child ($10.00)   _____
Forgiveness: Returning to the Original Blessing ($10.00)   _____

POSTERS AND NOTECARDS

Risen Christ Poster 11"x17" ($10.00)   _____
Ecstatic Moment Poster 8.5"x11" ($5.00)   _____
Risen Christ Notecards with envelopes 8/pkg ($10.00)   _____
Ecstatic Moment Notecards with envelopes 8/pkg ($10.00)   _____

SHIPPING

($2.00 for first item, $1.00 each additional item.
Add additional $1.00 for first class postage.)
MA residents please add 5% sales tax.   _____
                                                                    _____

                                        TOTAL   **$____**

Send Order To: Heartways Press
P. O. Box 181, South Deerfield, MA 01373
Toll free: 1-888-HARTWAY• 413-665-0555

Please allow
1-2 weeks
for delivery